Magic for Non-Magicians

by Shari Lewis and Abraham B. Hurwitz
Edited by Leo Behnke

Published by J. P. Tarcher, Inc., Los Angeles

Distributed by Hawthorn Books

*To Ann Ritz Hurwitz who has mothered our talents
and helped us to husband our energy, and whom we
both love.*

Copyright © 1975 by Shari Lewis and Abraham B. Hurwitz
All rights reserved
LIbrary of Congress Catalog Card Number: 75-17014
ISBN: 0-87477-043-2
Manufactured in the United States of America
Published by J.P. Tarcher, Inc.
9110 Sunset Blvd., Los Angeles, Calif. 90069
Published simultaneously in Canada by
Prentice-Hall of Canada, Ltd.
1870 Birchmount Rd., Scarborough, Ontario

**Illustrated by The Committee:
Chuck Bennett
Peggy Yatabe
Gerry Taylor**

Table of Contents

Introduction by Shari Lewis

"And what does your Daddy do for a living, little girl?" Oh, how I loved that question. "My father is the official magician for the City of New York," I would answer—and he was. My dad, Dr. Abraham B. Hurwitz, was affectionately known by millions as Peter Pan, The Magic Man, and for 18 years was the magician in charge of the magic program for the New York City recreation division.

The reaction was always: *"I didn't know that New York City had an official magician!"* Inevitably my flip answer was, "Where do you think the money goes?" But I knew that Pop took his position very seriously.

In the 1930's, Mayor LaGuardia had recognized the value of magic and had selected my dad to incorporate the magical arts and puppetry into the recreational program of the Department of Parks.

And it wasn't easy for Dad or for the rest of the family, for that matter. During the Depression my father, like many others, was holding down two jobs at the same time; he was teaching at the Yeshiva University in New York City and working for the Department of Recreation. Actually, these two jobs were not as far apart as they might seem because, for years before it became fashionable, Daddy was fascinated by the potential of education through entertainment. He involved youngsters in mathematics through the magic of numbers, in chemistry through those tricks that turn milk to wine and ink to water. He helped shy children find their tongue through their magical patter and difficult children to channel their energies more productively. (I remember Daddy, at one of the Juvenile Halls, teaching a group of children how to pull money out of the air. A tough youngster came up to him at the end of the lesson and assured him that he loved magic, and that pulling money out of the air was even easier than stealing!)

v

I am pleased that magic has become so popular again this year, because Daddy has been a staunch supporter of the inherent values of magic all of his life, and I can see that the resurgency of the popularity of magic is a confirmation of his confidence. Daddy has written extensively about magic in all of the magic and recreational magazines and has received many many awards (among them the Supreme Knight Jewel from the Knights of Magic and also the Star of Magic plaque from the International Brotherhood of Magicians—which was awarded to Blackstone, Dunninger, Cardini, Dia Vernon, and other master magicians).

"So your father is a magician! Does he saw your mother in half?" I always retorted to jokesters who asked that question that Daddy did indeed used to do that trick, until one night he made a mistake and really did saw Mama in half. "Now she lives in Seattle and Portland," I would say. "Isn't that wild? One mother with two zip codes!" My mother was never particularly interested in magic. She was a classical musician, and was one of the music coordinators for the New York Board of Education. But she shared Daddy's intense interest in youngsters, and took over the job of handling my father's magic bookings and negotiations with relish. All through my childhood, Daddy spent equally as much time at his magic as he did at the University. And our house was always full of magicians.

I think all of this affected my sister more than it did me. She used to watch Pop make everything disappear and then say "Abra Ca Dabra" and bring it all back, and it must have been frustrating to her. One day when she was about three, we heard a loud noise from another part of the house. We ran toward it and found my sister standing over the john, dropping mother's jewelry into it, saying, "Abra Ca Dabra" and pressing the handle! She made the jewelry disappear all right, but even Daddy's magic couldn't bring it back.

Is there really such a thing as magic? Pop's definition of magic is much looser than mine. He considers it to include the odd and the unusual any novelty form that violates the rules of cause and effect. So when he introduced me to puppetry and ventriloquism, it was, in his terms, within the scope of "the magical arts."

My definition has always been very different. I consider magic the art of trickery—and you're not doing magic unless you're "fooling" the audience. For some reason, I've never had great confidence in my abilities in this area. This is probably due to the fact that Daddy is such an excellent magician, and I never felt that I could do it quite as well as he. (I never played the piano, in spite of the lifetime of lessons, and the reason is probably the same. Mother is such a good pianist, and I just didn't feel that I could beat either of them at their own game!) This didn't stop my folks. Daddy taught me magic, and that's what I did, early in my theatrical career. I was stopped when, one day, I pulled a rabbit out of a hat in a large theatre. A little boy at the back of the theatre yelled, "I know how you did that trick," and I made the mistake of yelling back, "Yeah—how?" And the boy very confidently informed the audience, "You've got a false bottom!"

Can anyone learn it? For me, magic was like a vaccination that wouldn't take. For some reason, I have never been able to retain magic and remember the moves the way I retain scripts and songs. So Daddy always selected the very simplest of the best professional tricks and taught them to me in the clearest way.

That's what this book contains. Tricks his non-magician daughter could learn—and tricks that would please the audience, and trick them into the belief that she was better than she actually was.

Just as old jokes are brand new to those who haven't heard them before, many of these tricks are so old that they are brand new—a number of the tricks in this book are tricks that Daddy learned 40 years ago, and have not been in vogue for the past 20 or 30 years.

I hope these tricks bring you great fun and as for profit, well just remember this: if you learn how to pull money out of the air, you don't have to list it on your tax return as additional income!

My Name Is Magic
by Abraham B. Hurwitz

My name is Magic, and I am everywhere. Since the beginning, I have been worshipped and feared, and all religions grew with me and from me. Some who have followed my path have been burned as witches and devils, while knowing me has made others priests, healers, even kings. My accomplishments are hailed in every ancient text. And even today, when you look behind many of the explanations of the scientists, you will find that I am there. My name is Magic and I am everywhere.

Many years ago, working with problem children in New York, I saw a magician performing for a group of my delinquent boys. I was envious of the attention they had given to him but to no other teacher or leader. I saw that his magic had a power that could be employed in working with those boys, so I, too, became a magician. For over 40 years I have practiced my craft as teacher and camp leader, playground director, orphanage administrator and as the official magician for the City of New York. That was a magical decision for me, and I will always consider it as the best one I ever made.

Magic has been for me, as it has been for the thousands of children and adults that I have taught it to, an immensely positive aspect of life. Magic is a creative way of thinking and doing. It breaks the monotonous chain of daily life and shows us that the world still contains the unexpected and the seemingly inexplicable. Even in today's age of scientific wonders, it still stirs the imagination and forces us to think again about the way things are and the way things happen. It keeps us open to the mysterious and the unknown. Magic stirs the imagination, and transports the magician and his audience into a world of fantasy.

Magic stimulates laughter and wonder, and as magic causes others to laugh, it helps us to laugh. It takes our minds away from introspection or problems that can't be solved, and focuses us in areas over which we do have control.

Magic delights people of all ages, the sick and the handicapped, the rich and the poor. It crosses all borders and speaks a universal language. And as a developer of personality, magic is astounding! It helps a person think on his feet, develop his command of language and gives him a sense of confidence. It builds the ego and establishes a rapport between people of different generations and nationalities.

Magic itself is a friend, a lifelong hobby of endless variety which gives one entrance into an age-old fraternity existing in all parts of the world. It fills one's leisure time with an inexpensive activity, with unlimited room for growth of technique and knowledge.

When they get together, Magicians are brothers of a kindred spirit who enjoy one another's company, have a common frame of reference and endlessly amuse and entertain each other with variations on familiar themes.

Magic is a teacher, a demonstrator of laws of physics and chemistry and of mathematics. It instantly attracts the attention and makes its point in a visually exciting fashion.

Magic is a constant source of new ideas, yet is easily learned and readily performed. Psychologists establish rapport with their patients through magic, salesmen get attention through magic, and teachers use it to excite the interest of their students. Everything in one's backgroud can be utilized in its practice.

With its novelty, surprise, variety, humor and challenge, magic recreates the wonderful world of the child where everything is fresh and new. Magic is the last stronghold of the imagination. As science makes wonders recede—magic will always be there.

My name is magic, and I hope that yours will be too.

Doing Impromptu Tricks by Leo Behnke

Magic is a paradox—it is and it isn't.

It can apparently suspend the laws of nature—but it needs the laws of science to succeed. A careless or sloppy performance will hurt a trick but care and practice make magic as popular today as it ever was.

It's all because people like magic and always want to be fooled. That is the strength of magic, you will always have an audience. People *want* you to fool them, to show them something they can't explain. Why they have this desire can be discussed, theorized and debated for days . . . but not here. This book is to help you entertain these people who want to see magic, so all of you can have fun.

We will, however, give you a few hints so your tricks will go smoother and gain you the reputation of being someone who can entertain, not just do a trick or two. These pointers are to help you understand how magic works and how to get the greatest effect from the simplest trick. They are to let you have fun, not turn you into a student, so we'll keep them to a minimum.

PREPARATION:

Many tricks that seem to be impromptu and done on the spur of the moment, actually require a certain amount of preparation. A lot of newcomers become apprehensive when they hear the word "preparation," but they shouldn't. An old and very true maxim of magic is, "If the trick fools the spectator, the method is worth it." As you perfect more tricks and see more reactions to your magic you will come to see the truth of that saying. So, be prepared!

Quite often, the preparation is very simple and can be done long before you actually perform the trick. As you learn more magic keep your eyes open for tricks you can set up and put into your wallet, purse, pocket or desk, for a later performance. It is said of Oscar Wilde that long before he was to go to a dinner party he would mentally review the other people who would be guests, topics of discussion that would undoubtedly be mentioned, and who would be seated next to him at the table. In this way he would be able to prepare the wittiest of sayings, or as they say in show business, rehearse his adlibs. Should you do any less with your magic?

X

In your spare moments during the day's discussions or at a party, experiment and notice how people will look you in the eyes and not at your hands when you ask them a direct question. Watch how their eyes will follow a moving hand away from a stationary one, or how they will react if you move their hand with yours but not if you just touch it. You will soon be aware of a whole new way of catching people's attention or diverting it.

SURPRISE:

You should never tell your audience what your trick is going to be before you try it. There are two very good reasons for this. One is that they don't know where you're going, so if you get slightly lost on the way they won't know it. For example, if you're looking for a selected card in the deck and temporarily can't find it, then you'll need some time to work your way out of the dilemma. But if you've just told them it is now going to be turned over in the center of the pack, you're in trouble!

The second reason is that a good magic trick is like a good joke, it takes you by surprise. If a spectator knows the coin is going to appear in the center of the handkerchief he doesn't get nearly the same thrill as when it suddenly happens.

So, once again, don't tell your audience what's going to happen, until it does!

PRESENTATION:

Each person in this world is different. Some people like to tell puns and can get away with them, others like puns but can't deliver them effectively. Some have the knack of telling tall stories and making them sound logical, while others have trouble getting the truth believed. Whatever your personality is, that should be your style for doing magic. The popular conception of a magician being a tall dark gentleman with a goatee and beguiling manner fits only about one man in a million. Your spectators know you by your everyday personality, so don't make them wonder about your sudden change to the mysterious. Keep the face and spirit they're familiar with, and they will enjoy your magic.

Some tricks can be done with a story, and some create a fun situation, but most are best when done as a new trick you've learned in your study of magic. Do each trick in a manner you feel is appropriate under the circumstances. However, to give you a hint about what might be woven around each trick we have put an opening line under the title of each trick, and a closing line at the end. Use these as guides for the way you present the trick.

Also, as you read the tricks, don't be surprised when you find out how simple some of the secrets are. Simplicity is the key to good magic. Edgar Allan Poe was absolutely correct when he pointed out that people tend to overlook the obvious, they almost always try to find solutions more complicated than they really are. The simplest way is always the best.

Also under the subject of Preparation, are Practice and Rehearsal. Practice is considered the amount of time and effort devoted to perfecting a movement, usually a secret one, so it works smoothly and perfectly. Rehearsal is doing an entire trick or routine as though you were doing it for an actual audience. They are equally important, so do both to give you the confidence and polish that will enhance your magic.

MISDIRECTION:

A movement or speech that focuses the audience's attention on something else at a critical moment is needed in almost every trick. It can be something as simple as two words spoken directly to a spectator, or can be as elaborate as a three-bar fanfare by a 16-piece orchestra. Most living rooms and offices lack the space for a band so we'll stick to the simpler methods for the magic in this book. To help you recognize these important moments we have underlined them in certain tricks. You will then see what they are and how they are an important part of the presentation.

Harry Kellar, a grand magician of the golden age of vaudeville and theatre, once said that if he stood at the footlights of a theatre he could misdirect the attention of the audience so an elephant could walk across the stage and no one would see it. It sounds unbelievable, but it could be done by certain master magicians; in fact, some of them have come very close by doing things almost as extraordinary.

Magic in Your Pocket

Double Your Money

"You've heard of elbow grease, but have you ever heard of elbow luck. . . ?"

THE ILLUSION:

You crumple a single dollar bill into a ball and rub it on your elbow for luck. Evidently it works, for the bill multiplies itself into two bills.

THE PREPARATION:

An extra dollar bill is wadded into a ball and secretly wedged between your collar and the back of your neck (**1**). A woman could put the bill behind a shirt or blouse collar, or under the band at the back of a halter neckline. Have a second bill in your wallet.

THE TRICK:

Remove a dollar from your wallet and show it to be a single bill. Crumple it into a round ball and hold it between the very tips of your left fingers and thumb. Remark that you have to rub it for luck and bend your right arm. As you rub the bill on your right elbow, the fingers of that hand secretly steal the hidden bill from your collar (**2**). When you have it, stop rubbing the first bill and look at it closely. Explain that it looks as though you didn't rub it enough and, lowering your right arm, you take the bill in your right fingers, adding it to the secret bill hidden there. Now double your left arm and in the same way, rub that elbow with the two bills held as one.

Bring your two hands together, grasp a bill between the fingertips of each hand, and pull your hands apart as though you were tearing a bill in two (**3**). Roll each one in your fingers for a second or two and then drop the bills separately on the table. Open them up, smooth them out, and put them away in your wallet as you offhandedly remark that this is one trick that certainly comes in handy at times.

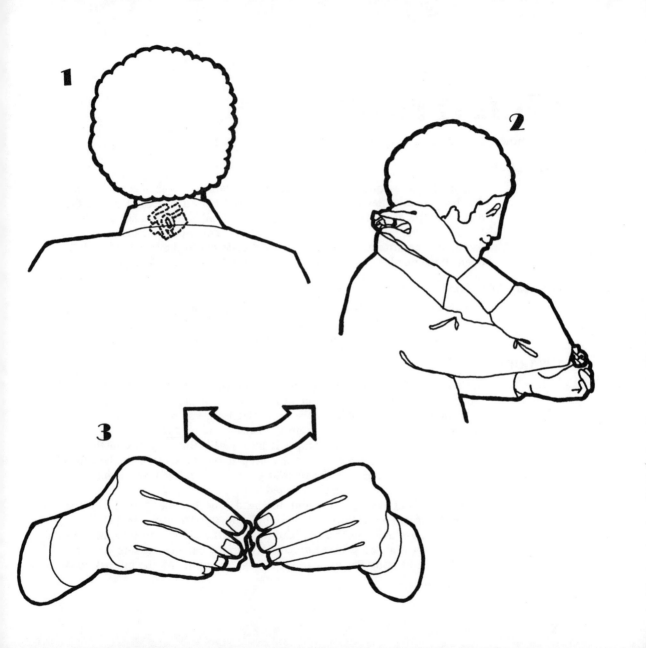

Pick a Buck

"You know, money doesn't always say 'Goodbye' when it talks to you . . ."

THE ILLUSION:

> Four or five one-dollar bills are tossed on the table and someone selects one. As this person writes the serial number of that bill on a piece of paper, the other bills are crumpled into wads. The selected bill is also wadded up, added to the others, and they're mixed together. You hold the bills to your forehead, one after another, and finally declare one to be selected bill. It is opened, the number checked, and you're absolutely correct. Amazing!

THE PREPARATION:

> A nickel that no one sees is your secret ally. Have this in your pocket, or if you're seated, in your lap, ready to secretly pick it up. Also make sure to have paper and a pencil handy along with five or six dollar bills.

THE TRICK:

> Scatter the dollar bills on the table and ask someone to select one. As he or she is writing down the serial number on a piece of paper, and as the rest of your audience are wadding up the remaining bills, you steal the nickel with your right hand. Take the bill from the person and read the number back to them for verification, then crumple it into a ball. But as you wad the bill wrap it around the nickel (1). Then drop it on the table with the other money. Have someone mix the wads as you turn your head so everyone can be sure you're not following the selected bill.
>
> As you hold the bills to your forehead, one by one, "to gather the personal emanations exuded by the bill," you squeeze each one (2). When you find one where you feel the hard lump of the nickel you very dramatically identify it as the selected dollar. Unwrap the bill, making sure you steal the nickel into your fingers without anyone seeing it. As the bill has been

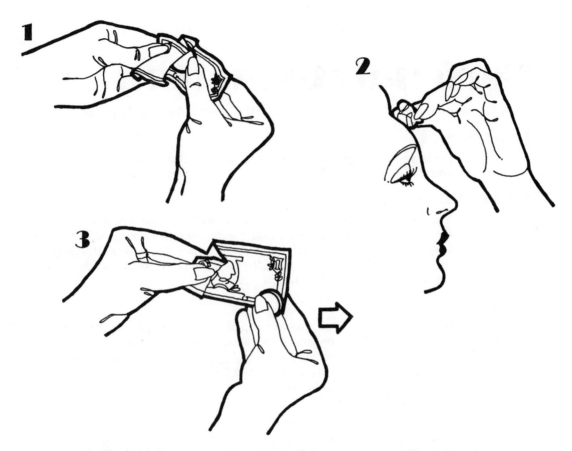

carelessly wadded up, your unwrapping will have to progress differently each time. <u>Pretend to be looking for the serial number</u> to cover your movements of unwrapping and stealing the nickel (3). Hand the opened bill to the person who is holding the written serial number. He or she will verify it as being correct, and you can claim to have exhibited an amazing feat of ESP. Who'll know?

Personal Magnetism

"Have you seen those photos of the electric energy that radiates from our fingertips. . . ?"

THE ILLUSION:

> Somehow you magnetize a cigarette just by making a circle around it with your finger. As you pull your finger away, the cigarette obediently follows it.

THE PREPARATION:

> You have to do a little practicing and the trick is strong enough to be worth the time. Place your head about twelve inches away from a cigarette and hold your lips slightly parted. Without pursing them, gently and quietly blow on the cigarette to make it roll along the table top (1). Practice making it roll at the same speed as your finger.

THE TRICK:

> Borrow a cigarette from someone and place it on the table in front of you. Rub your first finger on your sleeve, apparently to build up the static charge, and slowly draw a circle around the tabled cigarette. Do this three times, and then, as you draw the finger away from the cigarette, you gently blow on it so that it follows your finger (2).
>
> Ain't science wonderful?

Smoking Is an Expensive Habit

"I know someone who makes good money out of cigarettes . . ."

THE ILLUSION:

You prayerfully roll a cigarette between your two palms and it mysteriously changes into a dollar bill.

THE PREPARATION:

You prepare a cigarette by removing almost all of the tobacco. This is easily done by rolling the cigarette on the table making the tobacco squeeze itself out one end (1). Keep working toward this end and remove the tobacco until you have room for the bill in the hollow paper shell. There also will be a small plug of tobacco left at the other end.

Now the bill must be rolled tightly enough to fit into the cigarette. The fastest way to do this is to roll one end of the bill so that it becomes curled. Now moisten the palm of one hand and place the bill between your two hands with the curled end on the heel of that hand (2). Roll the bill in the direction of the curl and it will start rolling itself into a tight tube. When you get to the end of a stroke (when your two hands run out of rolling space) carefully place the bill back at its starting point and roll it again until it can be inserted into the hollow cigarette. Slide it into the paper tube as far as it will go, let go of it, and it will expand to fill the inside of the cigarette paper (3). Tamp down the plug of loose tobacco on the other end and you're ready.

THE TRICK:

Remove the prepared cigarette from your pack, surreptitiously wet your palms, and put it between your two palms. Rub the tube briskly and the thin paper will wad itself up into infinitesimal pieces of paper leaving just the bill. Open it, smooth out the wrinkles, and show the dollar bill—your profit for the day.

By the way, if you're using a filter cigarette, just be sure to tear off the filter end before you rub the wet cigarette between your hands.

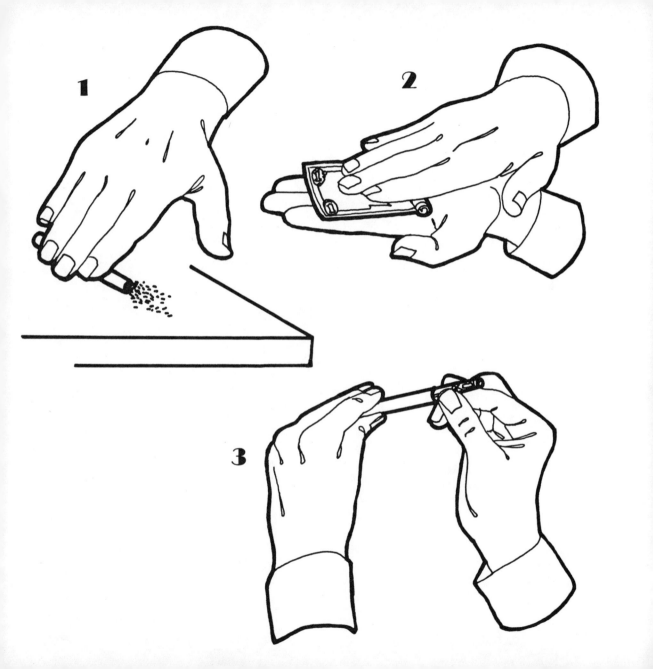

2

Magic Out of Your Purse

For Girls Only

"Here's proof that men are the weaker sex. . . !"

THE ILLUSION:

A chair is placed sideways to a wall and not quite touching it. A man leans over until his head rests against the wall, with his back straight and parallel to the floor, and with his feet spaced the same width as the chair. Now he has to lift the chair and then stand up with it. He utterly fails! However, every girl and lady in the room does it with ease!

THE PREPARATION:

The only preparation for this startling challenge is to be born a female! Women are able to lift the chair and stand because their hips are situated differently and provide a counterbalance to the rest of the body in that position.

THE TRICK:

Place an armless kitchen or dining room chair sideways to the wall and about an inch away from it. Have the man place his feet about an inch away from the chairlegs and spaced exactly the same distance apart. Tell him to place his hands as in the illustration and to lean over until his back is level and his head is resting against the wall (1). Now challenge him to lift the chair straight up (which is fairly easy) and then lift *himself* to a standing position while still holding the chair (which is impossible!) (2). Vive la difference! (3).

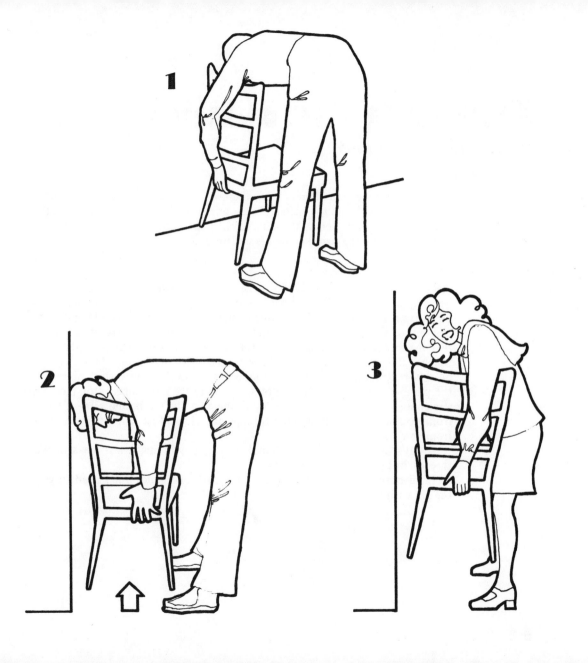

Through the Hanky

"Is it true handkerchiefs have a back door...?"

THE ILLUSION:

Someone holds a handkerchief by the two upper corners, and you put a safety pin through the top hem and near one corner. Suddenly, you move the pin in a straight line across the handkerchief to the other corner—but the pin is still closed and the handkerchief is undamaged.

THE TRICK:

Make sure your friend holds the corners of the handkerchief firmly and the hem tightly stretched. Push the safety pin through the cloth about a half-inch down from the hem and about three inches from the left corner (1). Take the coil end of the pin between your right thumb and fingers and twist the pin so that the moveable bar is on the right. Pull the pin towards you until the head touches the cloth, and your hand is to the right of the pin. Now, as you quickly pull the pin to the right, the material will slide between the point of the pin and the head (2). When you get close to the right corner stop moving, straighten the pin until it's at a right angle to the cloth, and push it away from you so it is again sticking through the cloth. Just like moving a chair from here to there (3).

Always use a relatively new handkerchief, as you might tear weak or old threads, but practice on an old one.

Incidentally, my father does this trick with one hand, but I need to grip the pin with two.

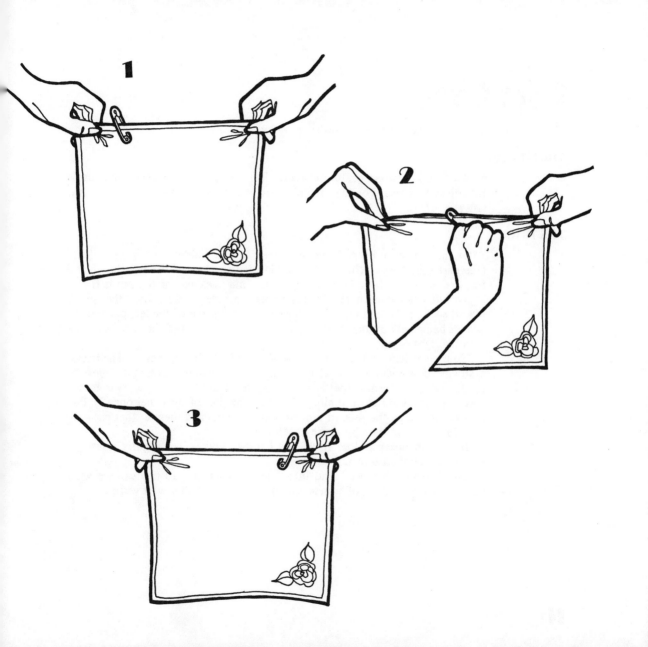

Pin Out

"Most people have to open a safety pin in order to remove it . . ."

THE ILLUSION:

Someone takes two large, unprepared, silver safety pins and fastens one inside the other. However, you take the pins and in a flash they are unlinked . . . but still closed!

THE TRICK:

After the pins have been linked and given to you, hold one with the coil end (the part that does not open) firmly between the ball of the left thumb and the first joint of the middle finger. The solid back bar of the pin is firmly supported from underneath by the tip of the index finger. The other pin is placed so that the coil end is resting on the upper bar of the left pin and the head is being held by the right fingers. Make sure that all of the right-hand pin is to the right of the left pin (**1**).

Your right hand must move in two directions at the same time. The first is a straight-down jerk of the right hand, as the second movement slides the right-hand pin toward the head of the left-hand one. These two moves together slide the right pin along the moveable bar of the other one (**2**). Pull that bar down so the second pin can unlink itself, and then let that bar snap back into its head thereby closing itself (**3**).

If the pin doesn't close itself, it's because you pulled slightly sideways, rather than straight down.

The two moves must blend into one to make sure no one can see what actually happens. And, of course, you have no idea at all how it works.

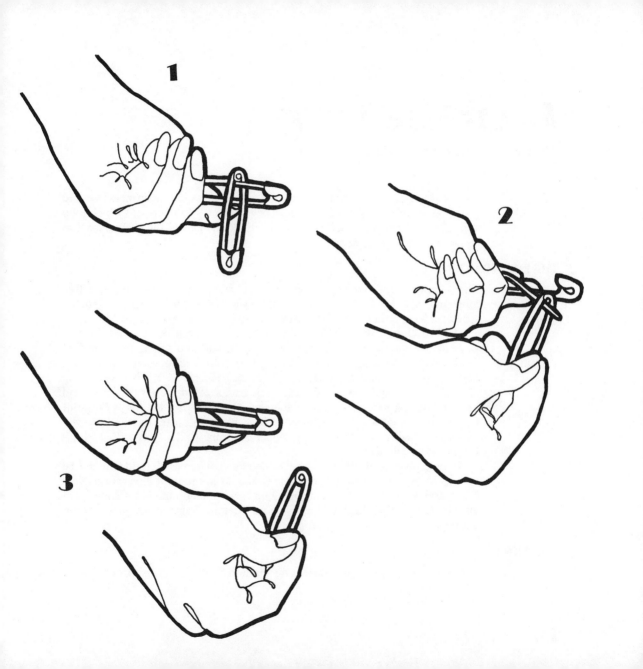

Loop the Loop

"Should a female con man be called a con person. . . ?"

THE ILLUSION:

You make a couple of simple loops on the table with a chain necklace and challenge people to beat a con game. They are to try to figure out which loop will *catch* their finger when you pull on the other end of the chain. Needless to say, they very seldom win.

THE PREPARATION:

There actually are two ways to arrange the chain. Method One has one free loop and one catch loop and Method Two makes two free loops—so the spectator loses either way! This gives you a slight advantage of 3 to 1!

Method One: Take a long neck chain and stretch it out so that the two sides of the loop are touching. Coil the right end in a spiral, as in the first illustration, making sure neither of the two strands crosses over the other. Pick up strand 3 and carry it over 2, placing it next to 1. Then slide 2 up alongside 4. Spread the loops until they are exact duplicates of the second picture, making sure that a bit of the chain extends past the loops (at point C). If the spectator puts his finger in loop B, he will lose, for the loop will NOT catch, when you pull the necklace at point C. Loop A *will* catch his finger and he will win.

Method Two: Coil the necklace in the same pattern as Method One but be sure to cross the two strands near the center, as in the third illustration. Now bring strand 3 over 2 to 1, and slide 2 up to 4. Open up the loops and you're set because neither loop will catch your friend's finger when you pull on point C.

THE TRICK:

Coil the necklace on the table using Method One and place your finger in

1

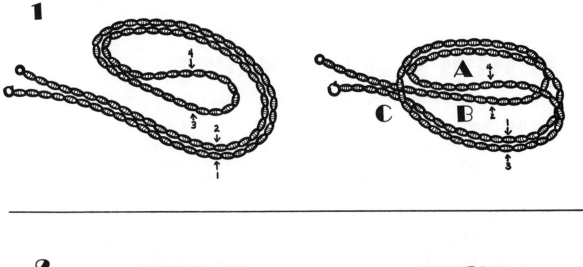

2

Loop A to show that it will catch your finger. <u>Use Method One again and ask your friend to put a finger in either loop.</u> Regardless of which loop is used, on the third time use Method Two. Use Method Two for about three times and then use Method One and place your own finger in Loop A to show that it can be done. No wonder con men always make so much money.

Jewelry Tomfoolery

"Through the ages, precious metals have been said to have magical qualities. . . !"

THE ILLUSION:

A solid bangle bracelet is threaded over both strands of a long chain necklace. Each end of the chain is then hooked over someone's index fingers. The challenge is to remove the bracelet from the chain while leaving the chain still looped over the two fingers . . . and surprisingly, you do!

THE TRICK:

With your right middle finger pointing down towards the floor place it on your side of the chain between the bracelet and the person's right finger. Pushing against that strand of the chain, lift it so you can transfer it to the other side of the chain. The two strands now make an X in front of and behind your middle finger (1). Put your right index finger in the loop on the side of the X to the left of your middle finger, slide your thumb down through the same loop as your middle finger, and put the tips of your index finger and thumb together. (Keep these two fingers tightly together until it's time to remove the bracelet.) Slide your right hand to the left and transfer the loop around your middle finger down onto the person's upright finger (2). Your left hand takes the strand of chain closest to you where it comes around the person's left finger, brings it all the way over to the person's right finger and drops the chain over it (3). Now take the bracelet in your left hand, separate your right finger and thumb, and take all of the fingers of your right hand out of the chain. When you pull on the bracelet it will come off the chain leaving it still looped over the fingers.

That was easy, wasn't it?

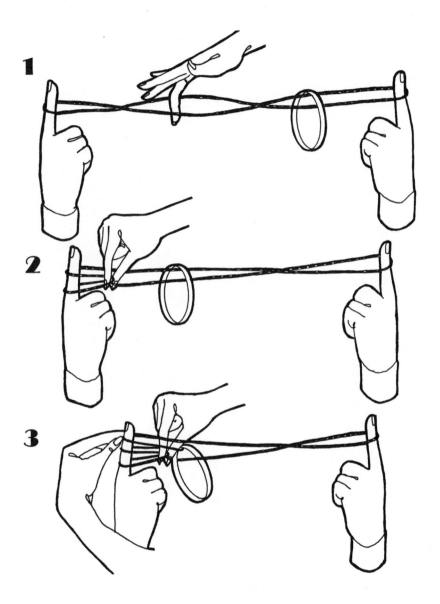

1

2

3

3

Magic at Your Desk

On and Off

"The rubber band is the world's greatest invention for wrapping around things. . . !"

THE ILLUSION:

Someone else threads a length of string through a rubber band, and holds both ends of the string very tightly. You cover the band with a handkerchief and make a few mysterious movements under the cloth. When you remove the handkerchief the band is now knotted around the center of the string. Reaching over, you very gently pull on the band and it comes completely free of the cord.

THE PREPARATION:

The one reason you are able to do the trick is the one thing your audience never suspects—the rubber band comes apart and goes back together.

Take a rubber band about two to three inches long and one-eighth of an inch wide and cut it through the center of either end with a sharp pair of scissors (1). Now put a small dab of rubber cement on the cut surface of each end and let it dry. Stick the two ends firmly together so you don't see any crack where it's been cut. Have ready a piece of string about two feet long and a handkerchief and you're all set.

THE TRICK:

Hand one end of the string to someone, thread the rubber band onto it, and give the person the other end of the string, too. As he holds the string stretched between his hands, cover it with the handkerchief (2). Now reach under the cloth and pull the two ends of the band apart. Remove the band from the string, press the two ends back together, and the cement will make them stick once again. Pull one end of the band around the string and push it through the loop formed by the other end (3).

Remove the handkerchief to show the band, <u>apparently now knotted onto</u>

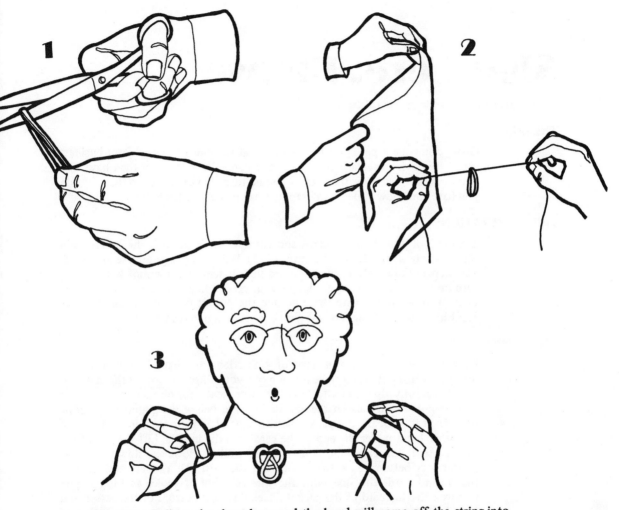

the string. Pull on the short loop and the band will come off the string into your hand. Do you think that was really magic or is that stretching it?

Sign Here, Please

"Criminals have a new technique called 'Instant Forgery'...!"

THE ILLUSION:

> Giving someone a pen, you have him initial the end of one of your business cards. Removing the card from its rubberbanded packet, you then have him write his first name on the back. When he turns the card over to the first side you have somehow added a written message just above his initials.

THE PREPARATION:

> Take one of your business cards and cut a V-notch through the center, as in the illustration; this is your "gimmick" **(1)**. Write a message on a second card, but keep all the words on the same end that matches your gimmick. Place this card on top of ten or twelve more of your cards and put your gimmick on top of it. Wrap a rubber band twice around the packet of cards making sure the band hides the cut edges of the gimmick. Have a pen ready and you're all set.

THE TRICK:

> Drop the packet of cards in front of your friend and hand him the pen. Ask him to put his initials on the card, and put your finger on top of the gimmick **(2)**. Apparently this is just to hold the cards steady for him but it also makes sure he puts his initials on the end of the card below the gimmick. After he has signed it, pick up the packet with one hand and slip your index finger of the other hand under the end of the card with the initials. Lift the end of the card so that you can remove it from the packet. However, slowly turn the packet over before you actually slide out the card **(3)**. You are now holding the second card, the one with the message, but it looks as though you removed the top card of the packet. Place this card in front of the person and have him write his first name across it, as you quietly drop the packet of

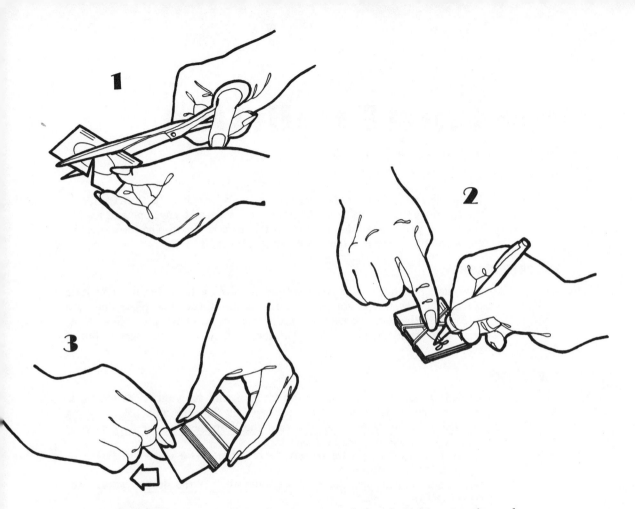

cards into a drawer. Take back your pen and then have him turn the card over. Surprise!

If he wants to examine the packet of cards you can very easily thumb off the gimmick as you remove them from the drawer.

Top Card Prediction

Have you ever heard of 'card pre-memory'. . . ?"

THE ILLUSION:

>One of your spectators removes a deck of cards from its case, shuffles it, cuts it, and places it on the table. She now opens a sealed envelope and reads a prediction you wrote long before. It is the name of a card. She turns over the top card of the deck and there is the very same card!

THE PREPARATION:

>You have previously stolen a card from the deck and written its name on a piece of paper which you seal inside the envelope. Now place that card underneath the envelope with its back against the envelope, and even with the edge you are likely to grab (1). Put the envelope and card together out of sight.

THE TRICK:

>Casually toss the deck of cards onto the desk and ask your friend to shuffle the deck. When she's finished and has replaced the deck, <u>nonchalantly bring out the envelope with the hidden card and drop them on the deck</u> so your card becomes the top card of the pack (2).
>>"In this envelope I have written a prediction. As a matter of fact, I wrote it three hours ago."
>
>With your finger, <u>flick the envelope sideways off the deck</u> towards your spectator (3).
>>"You shuffled the deck yourself and no one can possibly know any of the cards. Open the envelope and read what I have written inside."
>
>When she has read the prediction out loud, for the benefit of any other people watching, have her turn over the top card of the deck.
>>That's impossible, but it works!

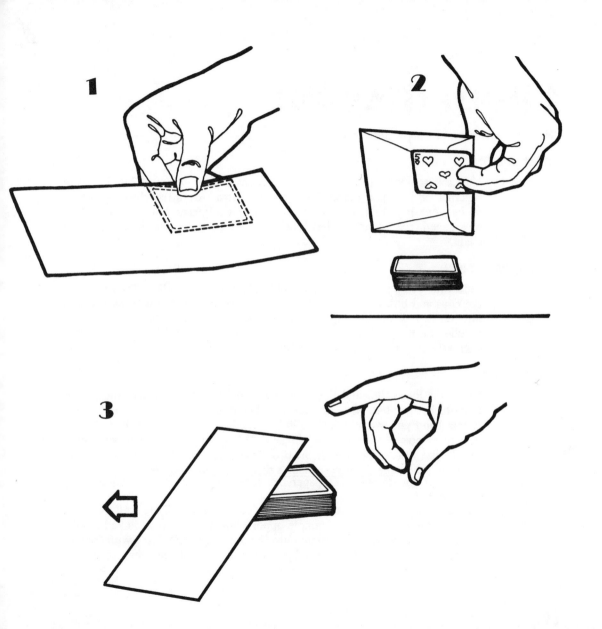

Clipped Again

"Have you ever been to a paperclip party. . . ?"

THE ILLUSION:

You ask someone to count some loose paperclips, then to bundle them together and wrap a rubber band around them. After the clips are placed under your friend's hand, you snap your magic fingers. When the bundle is unwrapped, the paperclips have magically linked themselves together into a chain.

THE PREPARATION:

Find fourteen paperclips and two rubber bands exactly alike. Take seven of the clips and link them into a chain, double them up (accordion pleat them) into the length of one clip, and wrap one of the rubber bands around the bundle (1). Keep the loose seven clips and the other rubber band in a small dish or box. Conceal the linked bundle of clips in a convenient spot.

THE TRICK:

Dump the loose clips and the rubber band in front of your friend and ask for them to be counted. While the clips are being counted and wrapped with the rubber band you secretly get the linked bundle in your right hand and cradle it in the crook of your last two fingers (2). Pick up the bundle of loose clips that he has just wrapped with the tips of the fingers of the right hand, and at the same time, <u>take the other person's right hand with your left.</u>

"I want you to cover the paperclips with your hand so they will be in the dark."

As you say, "I want you . . ." slightly lift his hand. They will shift his gaze to you which gives you ample opportunity to drop your linked bundle on the table and retain the loose clips in your fingers (3). Place your friend's hand right on top of the paperclips, pause a moment, and then snap your

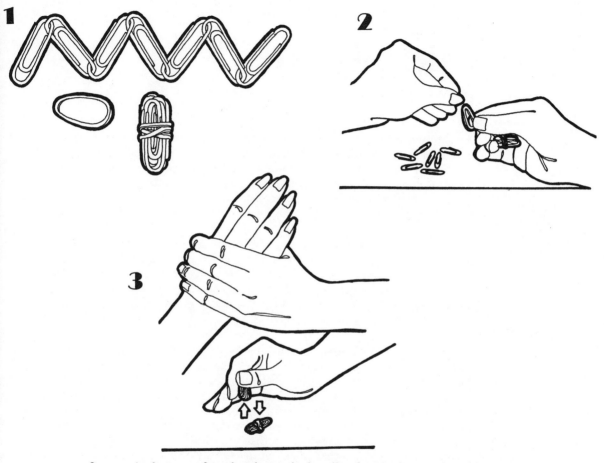

fingers. And as your friend picks up the bundle of paperclips on the table and unwraps them, you have plenty of time to casually drop the loose clips into your lap, a pocket, or the drawer of your desk.

Isn't it wonderful how paperclips stick together?

Jumping Coin

"Let me show you a new way to use your head . . ."

THE ILLUSION:

An empty matchbox is placed on top of someone's head and is balanced there as a coin is sealed inside an envelope. The envelope is placed on a second person's head who stands at least three feet away. A clap of the hands and the magic is done. The envelope is torn open and shown to be empty, and the missing coin is found inside the closed matchbox.

THE PREPARATION:

Push the drawer of a matchbox about two-thirds of the way out of its cover. Slide a penny into the opposite end of the cover and wedge it between the inner end of the drawer and the top of the cover (**1**). Prepare the envelope by slitting almost the entire length of one end with a sharp razor blade (**2**). Have a duplicate coin in your pocket and you're ready to do the trick.

THE TRICK:

Show the inside of the empty matchbox by holding it toward the audience and with the drawer rising above the cover, thumb on the bottom, fingers on the top. Close the box by gently sliding the drawer down into the cover (**3**). Ask someone to imitate a magician's table and as you place the box on top of his or her head, squeeze the sides of the box to free the coin. Remove the penny from your pocket, show it, and drop it into the envelope, making sure the slit end is held slightly higher than the other. Now as you seal the envelope tilt it in the other direction so that the penny secretly slides into your waiting fingers (**4**). Gently put the envelope on a second person's head to also use their talents as a table.

Clap your hands to create the magic force. Remove the envelope from "Table No. 2," tear off the slit end, and let the person examine the envelope.

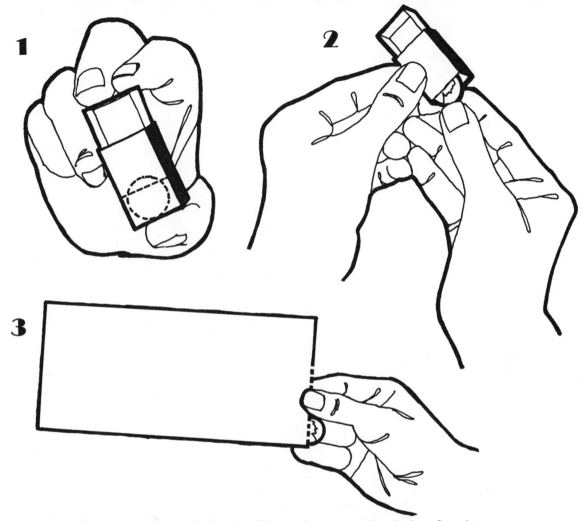

Without going near "Table No. 1" have the person take the box from his or her head and open it. There is the missing coin. Well, if *you* call it the missing coin, they'll believe you!

4

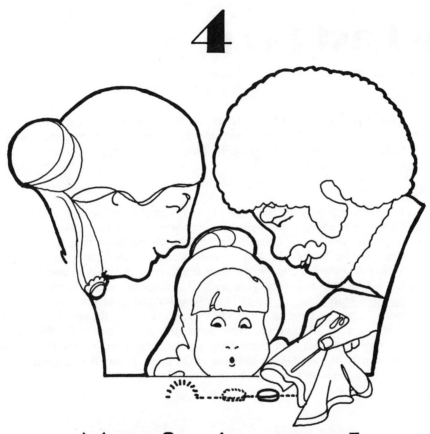

Magic Around
the Dinner Table

The Last Drop

"What exactly IS heavy water. . . ?"

THE ILLUSION:

You place a glass on a book, fill it half full of water, cover it with a napkin, and ask a woman to lift it. She does so easily. You add one more drop of water and ask her to lift it again. This time, however, she'll find it utterly impossible to lift the glass!

THE TRICK:

The book will be your tray. Hold it with your thumb on top, and your last three fingers underneath, supporting the weight of the book. Keep your index finger free but out of sight. Place the glass on the book so that it sets fairly close to your thumb (**1**). Pour in some water and then cover the glass with a napkin or handkerchief. When your friend grips the glass through the cloth she will be able to lift the glass with ease. Remove the handkerchief and add just one more drop of liquid. As you cover the glass this time bring your index finger out from under the book so you can grip the glass between your index finger and thumb (**2**). Now when your friend tries to lift the glass you can very easily keep her from doing so. Before you remove the handkerchief you merely put your finger back under the book. It may not be scientific, but that's the magician's version of heavy water!

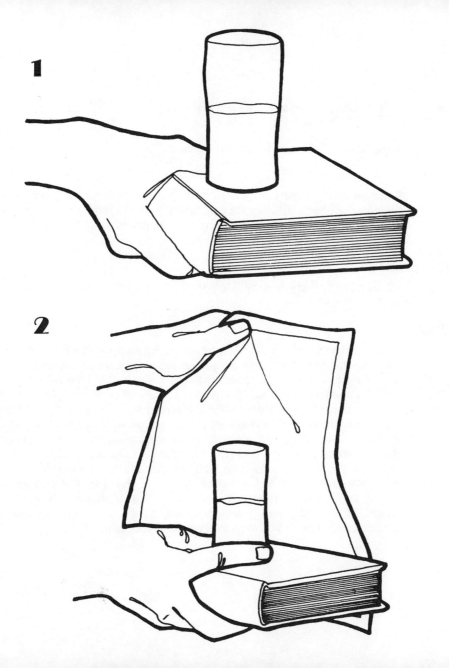

1

2

Tip of Your Toe

"You know, a magician is full of magic from head to toe. . . !"

THE ILLUSION:

Someone freely selects a card from a shuffled deck and it's cut back in amongst the others. To keep the cards away from the food, the deck is placed on the floor, and when you nudge it with the tip of your toe, the pack cuts itself right at the selected card!

THE PREPARATION:

All that is necessary is to spill a little salt or pepper on the table near you, before you start.

THE TRICK:

Have someone select a card and remember it. Square up the deck and place it on the table in front of you. As the person shows his card to the other people, press the tip of your index finger into the spilled salt (1). Press hard enough so that a number of the salt grains stick to the end of your finger. Don't wet your finger first, keep it dry. When the card is ready to be returned, tap the top card of the deck with your index finger <u>as you ask them to put it right on top</u> (2). You have just left a few grains of the salt on top of the pack. After the selected card is on the deck, have someone cut the cards and complete the cut. Now you place the deck on the floor. Ask for the name of the card, and then gently nudge the deck with the toe of one shoe (3). The deck will spill slightly and, because of the grains of salt, will cut itself somewhere near the center. Pick up the card below the break in the cards and you have the selected card. Haven't you even seen sleight-of-foot before?

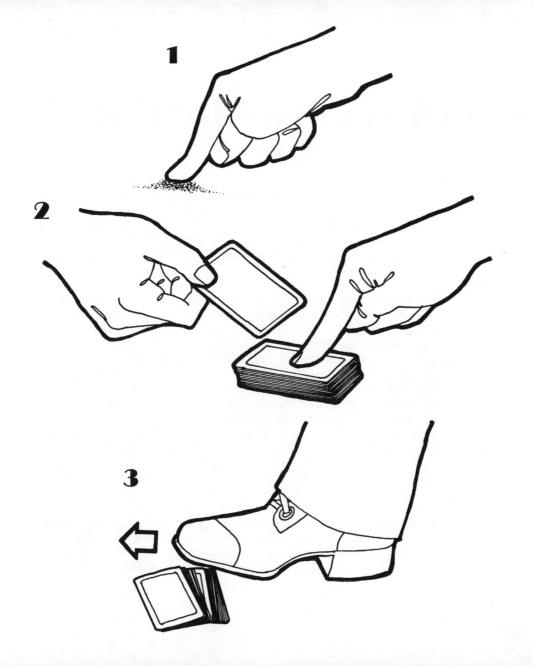

Goodbye, Mr. Lincoln

"Have you ever heard the phrase, 'The closer you watch. . .' ?"

THE ILLUSION:

You claim to be able to make a coin vanish. You cover the coin with a salt shaker, the salt shaker with a paper napkin. A snap of the fingers and you raise the salt shaker; the coin is in plain view. Another snap of the fingers and when you raise the shaker again the coin is still there. Finally, you hit the shaker with the flat of your hand and the entire salt shaker has vanished!

THE TRICK:

Put a penny on the table about eighteen inches away from you. Place a salt shaker on top of the coin. Cover the shaker with a paper napkin. (Preferably, the napkin should be folded in quarters. If it's not large enough to cover the shaker, open it one fold.) Running your hand down the shaker will form the paper to the shape of the shaker (1). Announce your intention of making the coin disappear. Snap your fingers, lift the shaker by squeezing the sides of the paper, and bring the shaker toward you, almost all the way to the edge of the table. Shake your head at the coin refusing to leave when you asked. Now you will have to command it. Replace the shaker over the coin. Snap your fingers and again lift the shaker. This time you bring it all the way to the edge of the table and let the bottom of the napkin extend slightly below that edge. As you reach over with your other hand and turn over the coin you simultaneously relax your grip on the paper, which will allow the shaker to drop into your lap (2). Gently replace the empty napkin, still holding its shape of the salt container, over the coin. Tell them you're going to try something else and slam your hand down on the empty paper (3). Pause no longer than a second, then reach over and flick the flattened napkin away to reveal the coin. Commenting on how stubborn Abe Lincoln could be, ignore the fact that you have vanished the salt shaker. Your audience won't!

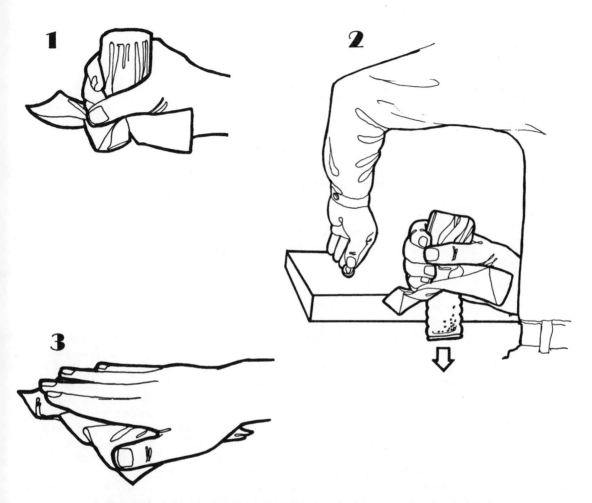

1

2

3

Oh, yes, before you leave the table don't forget to slip the shaker back onto the table. There isn't any special way. You will have lots of opportunities so take advantage of one.

Fadeaway Dime

"Are magicians to blame for the shortage of coins in America. . . ?"

THE ILLUSION:

A dime is fairly and openly folded into a cloth napkin. Nevertheless, when the napkin is shaken out the dime has vanished.

THE PREPARATION:

In one corner of your napkin about one inch in from the sides, you put a very very small piece of either soft chewing gum, or sticky soap. Have a dime handy.

THE TRICK:

Spread the napkin out flat on the table or on the palm of the spectator's hand so that the two corners nearest to you drape just over the edge. The piece of gum or soap is on the upper surface of the cloth, in the right corner near you (1). Place the dime in the center of the napkin. Pick up the lower left corner and cover the dime with it. Ask someone to feel the dime through the cloth. Uncover the coin, opening the corner of the cloth all the way out. Pick up the dime, show it again, and replace it in the center. Now pick up the prepared corner and bring it to the center, so the sticky substance rests on top of the coin. Press down on the dime. Bring in the other three corners to cover the dime, and ask someone to feel the coin again (2). Reach into the pile of corners and pick up the one that came from the upper left. Very openly, with just the thumb and finger, pull that corner out and the handkerchief up and away from the table so that the dime doesn't hit the surface. Gently wave the hanky a couple of times to prove the dime has vanished and then run it through your hand. As your hand gets to the bottom corner you steal off the coin into your fingers (3). Toss the handkerchief out for examination and you can pocket the dime. You've just discovered another neat way to get rid of money.

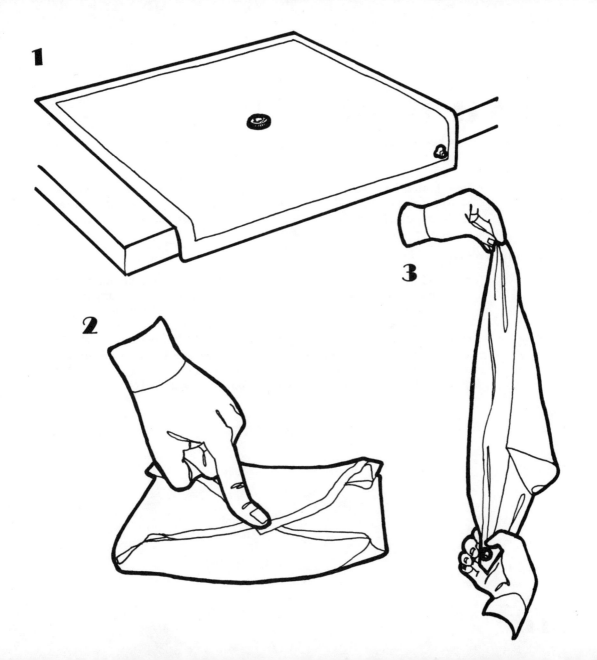

It's a Steal

"In the Orient they have ceremonies for everything . . ."

THE ILLUSION:

> Your hostess loans you an empty candy dish which you set in front of you. A napkin is shaken out and proven to be absolutely empty. The corners of the cloth are gathered up, the dish thrust up into the folds, and when you remove it candy or nuts fill it to overflowing!

THE PREPARATION:

> A second napkin is needed, one that you prepare ahead of time and smuggle in to your place at the table. (It can be inside your jacket, in your purse, or preset under the table at your chair.) Follow the folding diagrams and after you've tied the knot (4), put a quantity of nuts or candy inside the bag, pushing it all the way to the top. Now bring up the bottom corner, fold the left side past the center, and bring the right corner over to lock inside the left one, as (8). Finally, shake the goodies down into the bottom of the bag. The pressure of your load inside should keep your "load bag" locked shut.

(Continued)

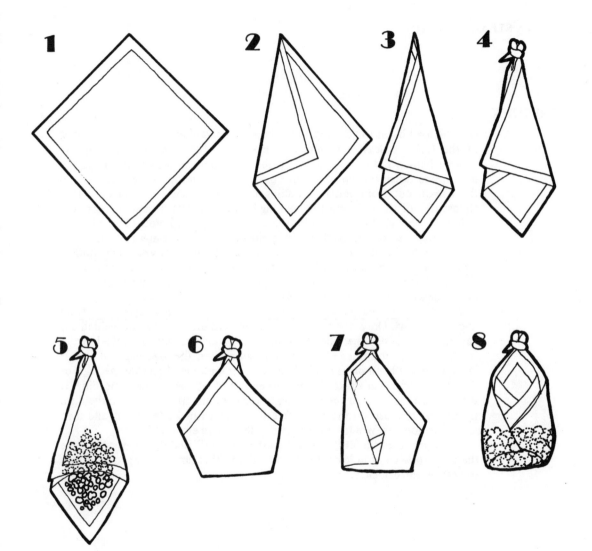

THE TRICK:

Get the load bag into your lap, with the knot upward and just below the edge of the table, at least a minute before you ask for an empty dish. Spread another napkin flat in front of you with one corner toward you (9). Place the dish upside down on top of it. Put your left hand on top of the dish and pull the napkin out from under it, pulling the cloth straight to you until it is almost free of the dish and then pulling it upwards (10). This time, cover the dish with the napkin, and hold the corner closest to you (11). Lift the opposite corner of the napkin with your left hand and bring it back to the corner you're holding (12). Turn the dish rightside up as your right middle two fingers take hold of the knot of the load bag in your lap. As soon as you have the bag securely between them your left hand replaces the outer corner of the napkin, covering the dish (13).

Now use the same move you did when you pulled the napkin out from under the bowl. Only this time you are bringing the load bag up behind the napkin at the same time. The attention of the audience will be on the bowl in front of you as the folds of the napkin fall around the load bag and hide it (14). Your left hand picks up the dish, takes it underneath, inside the folds of the napkin, and you shake the napkin and the load bag at the same time. It should open the folds of the load bag so the contents spill down into the dish. If not, put the dish on the table, free the folds with the left hand, and then reveal the goodies. Wouldn't it be great if they were emeralds?

After you pass the dish down the table you will find it very easy to untie the knot so when you leave the table both napkins can be dropped on others to destroy the evidence.

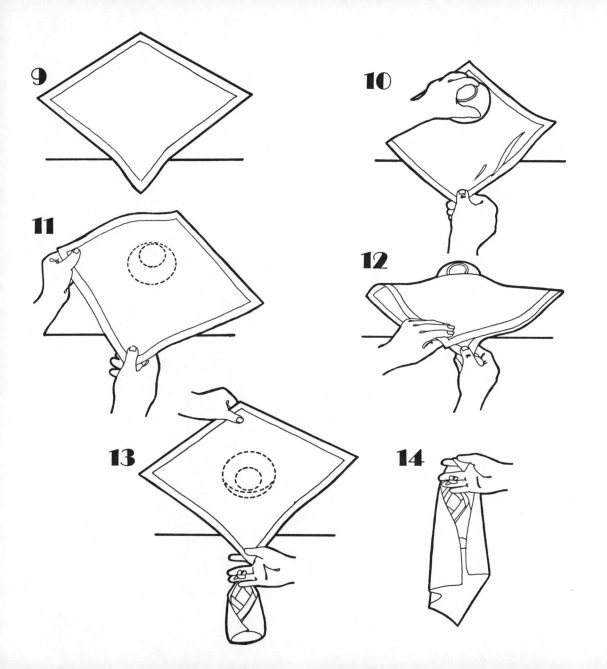

Magic at the Bar

Classic Peanut Trick

"Where do peanuts go in the winter time. . . ?"

THE ILLUSION:

>Three lonely peanuts are on the bar. You pick up two of them and openly drop them into your empty left hand. The third peanut is swallowed. Amazingly though, when you open your hand there are the three peanuts!

THE PREPARATION:

>A minute or so before you do the trick, take a peanut and wedge it between the middle and ring fingers of your right hand. Let the fingers relax and they will curl into a perfectly natural look (**1**).

THE TRICK:

>Put three peanuts in a row in front of you. With your right fingertips, pick up one and drop it into your cupped left hand. A second nut is picked up and you drop it and the secret peanut together into your left hand which immediately closes (**2**). Don't move your right hand away from your left the second time any faster than you did the first time. Wiggle the left closed fingers a little, open the hand, and roll three peanuts out onto the bar (**3**). Nothing like having your peanut and eating it, too!

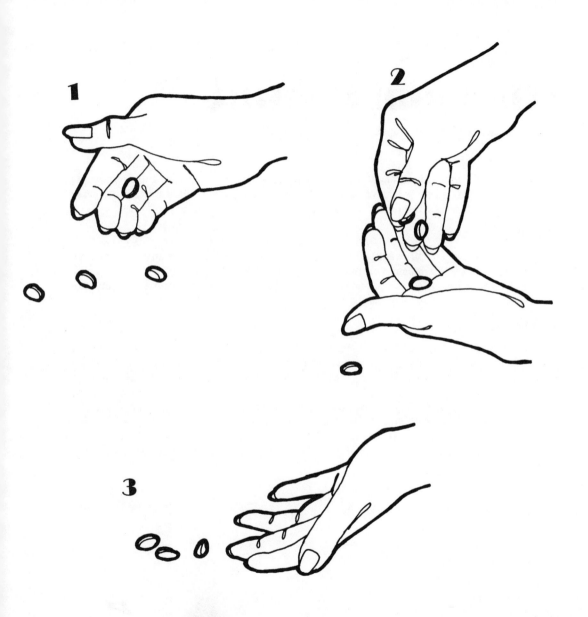

The Final Peanut

"Being the last doesn't always make you the loser...!"

THE ILLUSION:

A contest is arranged between you and a friend. You take turns removing as many as six peanuts at a time from a pile on the bar. The winner is the person taking the last peanut. Needless to say, you always win.

THE PREPARATION:

There are 30 peanuts on the bar. If you each can take as many as six nuts at a time, this means you must remember the key numbers of 9, 16, and 23 (1). Each time your opponent removes peanuts, you must remove as many more to total your key numbers.

THE TRICK:

Let's say the sucker, I mean, your worthy adversary, takes four peanuts for his first move; then you remove five more to make a total of 9 (2). On his second turn if he takes, say, five, you slide out two of them to bring the total to 16 (3). If his third turn nets him three, you take four, to get to your last number of 23 (4). Now no matter how many or how few he removes, you can easily take the rest to win the "game." If your bar buddy asks you to go first, only take one or two peanuts. Then, no matter how many he takes, on your next turn make sure that a total of 9 are gone. All that work just for peanuts!

1

2 9

3 16

4 23

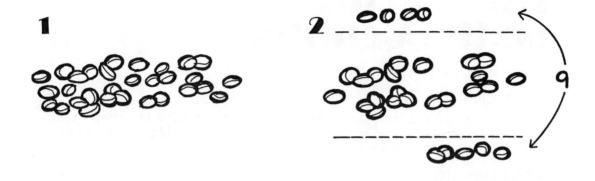
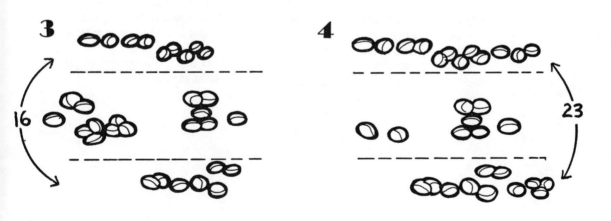

Three Coins on the Counter

"I'm sure you've heard the phrase, 'Pick them up and lay them down' . . ."

THE ILLUSION:

As you alternate picking up and laying down three coins you manage to put the last coin down on a count of ten. No matter how hard your friend tries he always gets stuck with coins in his hand.

THE PREPARATION:

When you do the trick, you must start with the coins on the bar. When you ask your friend to try it you put the coins into his hands so he starts the trick backwards.

THE TRICK:

Point to the three coins lying in front of you **(1)**. Pick them up one at a time, "One, two, three . . ." Now lay them down, ". . . four, five, six. . . ." **(2)**. Pick up the first two, ". . . seven, eight . . ." just point to the last one on the bar, ". . . that's an extra one . . ." **(3)** and then put down the ones in your hand, ". . . nine, . . . and ten" **(4)**.

Now pick up the coins, put them into his hands, and challenge him to get all three coins on the table with a count of ten. Looks as easy as 1, 2, 3!

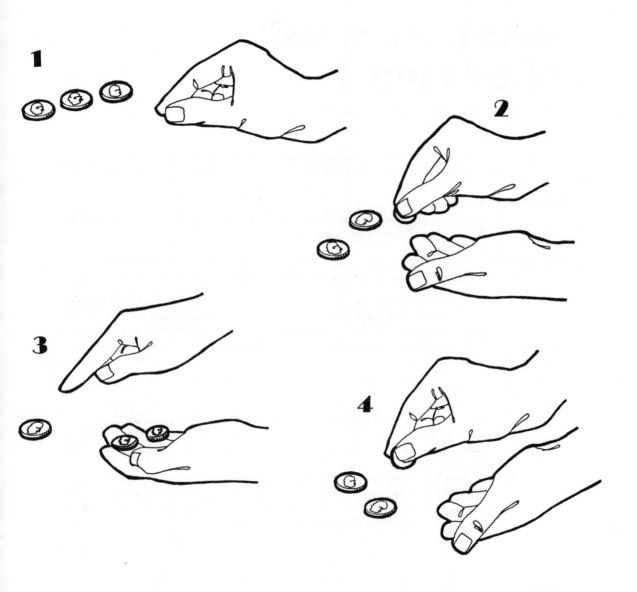

Making an Ash of a Friend

"I promise, this trick won't be a sobering experience. . . !"

THE ILLUSION:

You very openly mark someone's palm with a spot of cigarette ash. The mark is rubbed carefully and some of the ash magically appears on the other hand!

THE PREPARATION:

Before starting the trick you have secretly touched the tip of your left middle finger in an ashtray to get some ash on it (1).

THE TRICK: "Before we begin I must test you for steadiness. Hold both hands straight out in front of you, fingers open flat, and palms down."

When the person does so, take his left hand in your right and his right in your left, with your thumbs on top and fingers underneath, and raise his hands <u>about six inches</u> (2). At the same time, press the tips of both middle fingers into his palms, thereby marking his right palm with the ash on your left middle finger.

"No, a little higher . . . there, that's good. Now wiggle the fingers of either hand."

If he wiggles his left hand say, "All right, we'll use that one. Close the other one and put it under your left armpit." If he wiggles the marked hand, tell him, "That one? Good, close it into a fist and put it under your other armpit."

· Now have him turn over the unmarked palm as you openly dip the tip of your left middle finger in the ashtray. Solemnly make an ashy spot on the palm of his open left hand and gazing at it very seriously, start rubbing it with your thumb (3). After five or six seconds stop rubbing.

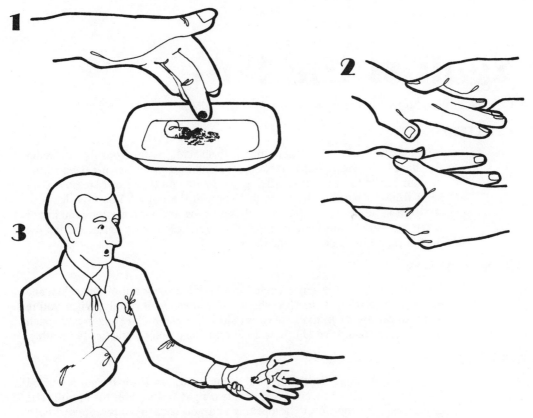

"Have you noticed how the mark has lost some of its substance; it looks lighter, doesn't it? Do you know why? No, it's not that . . . open your other hand."

He will open his closed right fist and discover that part of the ash has jumped from one hand to the other. If he thinks that's something, he ought to see your trained pink elephant.

Against the Law

"Even the smallest bottle has a teeny-weeny genie in it. . . !"

THE ILLUSION:

You borrow an open bottle of liquid (beer, cola, soda) from the bartender and hold it between your two hands, top and bottom. Reversing the position of your hands to bring the bottle upside down, you then slowly remove your hand from its mouth, and the liquid stays in the bottle! You even let your audience look closely at the neck of the bottle and they see the liquid right up to the mouth, but there it stops! Then you hold it over a glass and tap the bottom, and out comes the liquid!

THE PREPARATION:

Long before, you have cut a circle the size of a quarter out of the cellophane of a cigarette pack. Have this where you can get to it readily. When you're ready to do the trick, moisten your right index and middle fingers and touch them to the cellophane (1). It will stick to them and be practically invisible.

THE TRICK:

Take a small, filled bottle in your right hand, set it on the outstretched fingers of the left, then put your first two right fingers over the mouth. The cellophane goes right over the opening and you change the positions of both hands slightly to turn the bottle upside down. Close your left fingers to grip the bottle by its sides. At the same time, spread your two right fingers against the mouth of the bottle to make a good seal (2). Remove your right fingers and the liquid will remain in the bottle. If you have cut your circle the right size, you can inspect the mouth closely and still not see the cellophane. After you've proven your magical point, hold the bottle over an empty glass or pitcher and tap the bottom. The liquid and cellophane will drop into the container and no one will ever find your gimmick (3).

"Thank you, teeny-weeny genie . . . actually, she prefers diet drinks!"

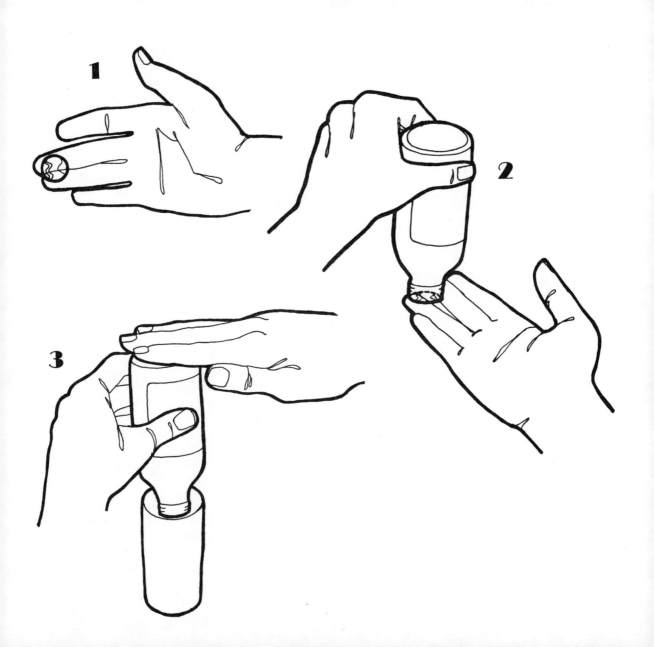

6

Magic Especially for Kids

Down the Chute

"Keeping track of money is very difficult. . . !"

THE ILLUSION:

A coin is placed in a square of paper and carefully wrapped up. You give a snap of the fingers and then tear up the paper to show that the coin has vanished.

THE PREPARATION:

There are two ways of doing this trick: Method One is entirely impromptu, and the other has a small amount of preparation. Both use a piece of paper about 4" square. For Method Two you prefold the paper into thirds, both horizontally and vertically, and cut a slit with a razorblade through one of the folds of the center section of the paper.

THE TRICK:

Method One—Place a coin in the center of the paper as you hold the paper in your hands, not on a table. Fold up the bottom third to cover the coin, and fold the top third down over that (1). Turn the paper a quarter-turn and, as you fold the top third down over the center section of the paper, let the coin slide out the bottom opening into your waiting fingers, which conceal it (2). Fold up the bottom third and hold the packet in the hand without the coin. Snap the fingers of your other hand then tear the packet in half to show that the coin has vanished.

Method Two—Place the coin in the center of the creased paper and fold up the bottom third. As you fold down the top third, let the coin slide down through the slit and into your fingers (3). Fold the left and right sections to the center and you're ready to tear up the empty packet. See what I mean?

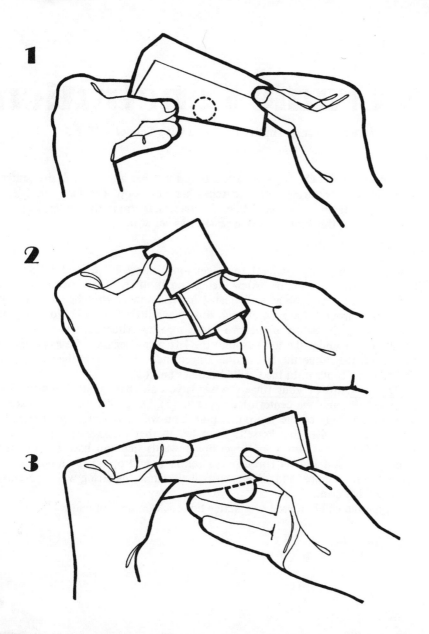

Cat's Cradle Penetration

"Ancient Egyptians said there was magic in the loops of a Cat's Cradle. . . !"

THE ILLUSION:

You make a Cat's Cradle, and have a friend put her arm through the center. You pull on the string, and it catches her in a loop. Leaving your friend caught, you again make the Cradle; she places her arm in the center, and you pull. However, this time the string penetrates her arm!

THE TRICK:

Tie a piece of string (at least four feet long) into a loop. Stretch the loop between your two thumbs, palms facing one another. Then stick your little fingers up into the loop as well. The string will now be stretched across your palms, and around the back of each thumb and little finger (1). To make the Cradle, bring the palms of the two hands together, slide the tip of the right middle finger under the loop around the left palm, separate the hands about six inches, then slide the left middle finger under the loop on the right palm. Separate the hands until the Cradle becomes taut (2).

Turn the tips of your fingers towards you and have your friend put her hand UP through the center of the Cradle (3). Drop all your fingers except your thumbs out of the loops and pull. You will have caught your friend's wrist. Don't let her free herself. Keep her in that loop, and make another Cradle. This time turn your fingertips towards her and have her put her imprisoned hand DOWN through the center (4). Drop all the loops except around your thumbs, and when you pull this time the string will apparently penetrate her arm.

"Egyptian children used to practice this trick on their mummies."

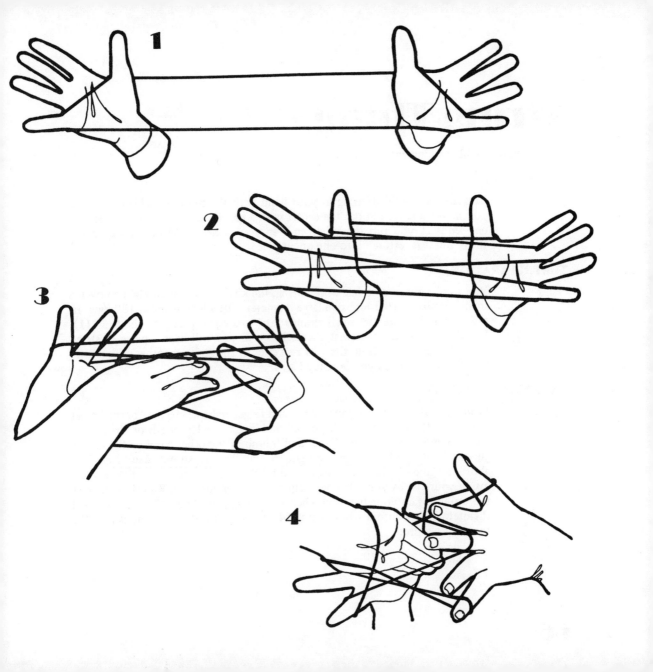

String Thing

"I never have trouble making ends meet. . . !"

THE ILLUSION:

You hold a length of string in your hand with the center hanging down, and you have someone cut out the center with a pair of scissors. He holds the two new ends as you rub the other ends in your hand. Suddenly you drop the string and it is restored into one uncut piece.

THE PREPARATION:

You need a piece of thick white string, the kind consisting of eight to twelve small strands twisted into one large diameter. Cut a length about 18" long. In the center separate the small strands into two equal parts for about 3" (1). Let the two sections retwist themselves and you will have a piece of string with "horns" on it. Glue the two real ends of the string together with a little bit of white glue and you're ready (2).

THE TRICK:

Hold the string between your thumb and finger right where the "horns" meet the string. It looks as though you are holding a regular length of string near the two ends. Put the first finger and thumb of the other hand on the dab of glue and pull the loop of string tight so that the two strands can be cut just above the glue (3). Have the string held by the two new ends. Put the "horns" inside your fist as you ask your helper to pull on his ends. Rub the center of the string inside your fist, and when you let go, the "horns" have retwisted themselves back into a whole string (4). Once again Magic triumphs over the forces of Nature.

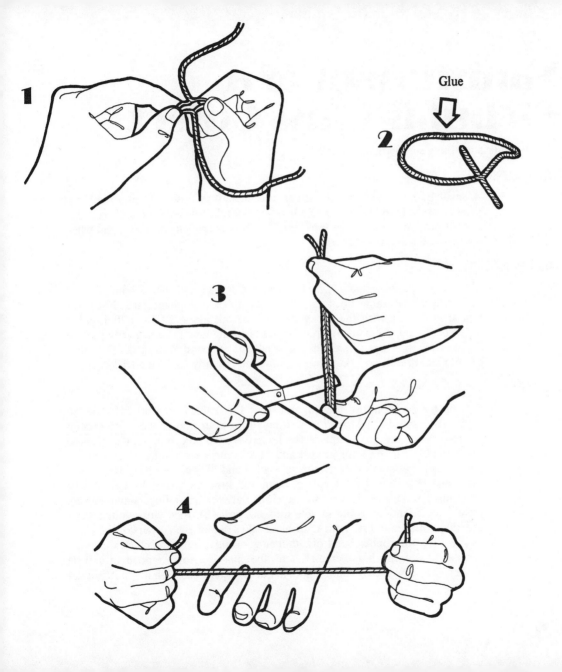

1

2

Glue

3

4

Vanishment of a Globular Glass Object

"And now for something simply marble-ous!"

THE ILLUSION:

A small box is shown to be empty and then it is closed. Then a marble is placed carefully in the center of a handkerchief, but when the handkerchief is shaken out, the marble has vanished. The box is shaken, it rattles, and when opened you roll out the marble.

THE PREPARATION

You need a handkerchief, two identical marbles, a small rubber band, a small box with a removable lid, and a short length of cellophane tape. Form the tape into a circle with the sticky side on the outside and press it flat on the inside of the lid. Press one of the marbles onto the tape (1) and gently put the lid back on the empty box. Put the small rubber band around the first joint of your left middle and ring fingers. Now you're ready to do the trick.

THE TRICK:

Pick up the box, remove the lid, and show the inside of the box. Handle the lid casually and don't look at it, <u>putting all the attention of the spectators on the *bottom* of the box.</u> Replace the lid and set the box to one side. Take the other marble out of your pocket and have someone examine it carefully as you spread the handkerchief over your left hand. When your hand is covered, slide your thumb under the rubber band and stretch it open. With your right first finger poke a little well in the cloth between your fingers and thumb. Have your friend drop the marble into the well (2), then close your fingers and the cloth around it. Your right hand takes one of the corners of the cloth as you slide the rubber band off your fingers and around the cloth above the marble. Shake the handkerchief, and the marble, now trapped in a little pocket, has apparently vanished (3). Put the handkerchief in your pocket

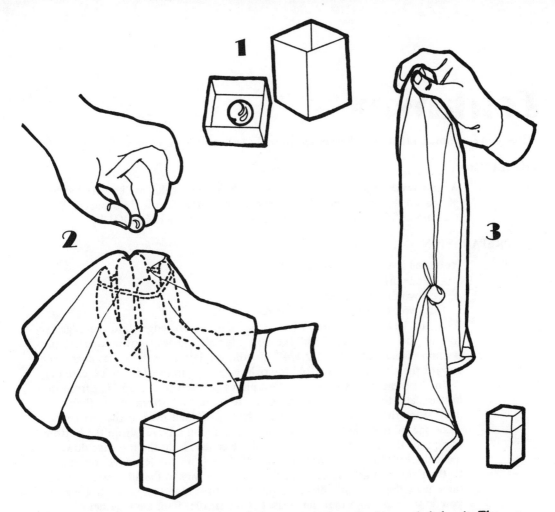

with your left hand as your right hand picks up the box and shakes it. The marble will come loose from the tape and make a rattling sound; you can now open the box and roll it out.

"I've found the real meaning of shake, rattle, and roll."

Foldaway

"Have you ever noticed that magicians never do tricks with their own money?"

THE ILLUSION:

A borrowed coin is placed on a piece of paper, which is then folded and placed on another paper. Both papers are folded into a third paper. When they are unfolded, the coin has vanished and in its place is an IOU!

THE PREPARATION:

You need five sheets of plain paper.

Cut one into an 8-1/2" square.

Cut two into 6-1/2" squares.

Cut two others into 4-1/2" squares.

Take the largest piece and 2" up from the bottom edge, fold the edge up toward the center (1). Fold the top edge all the way down to meet the bottom crease (2). About 2-1/4" in from the left edge, fold that edge over toward the right (3). Then fold the right edge over to meet the left crease (4).

In the same way, the two smallest pieces are each folded up 1/2" from the bottom, and the top edge brought down to meet the bottom crease; then over 3/4" from the left edge, with the right edge folded over to the left crease. Take one of the middle-sized pieces and, at a point 1-1/2" from the bottom edge, fold the bottom edge up toward the center. Fold the top edge down to meet the bottom crease. At a point 1-1/2" in from the left edge fold it over to the right, and then fold the right edge all the way to the left crease. Do the same with the other middle-sized piece and then glue them back to back. As you do so, make sure that the creases of the smaller flaps are together (5).

Open the two sides of the middle-sized sections and put one of the smallest sections in each one. However, each of the smallest sections is turned over so its solid back is uppermost when you fold the middle section over it. The middle section is then folded inside the large section.

(Continued)

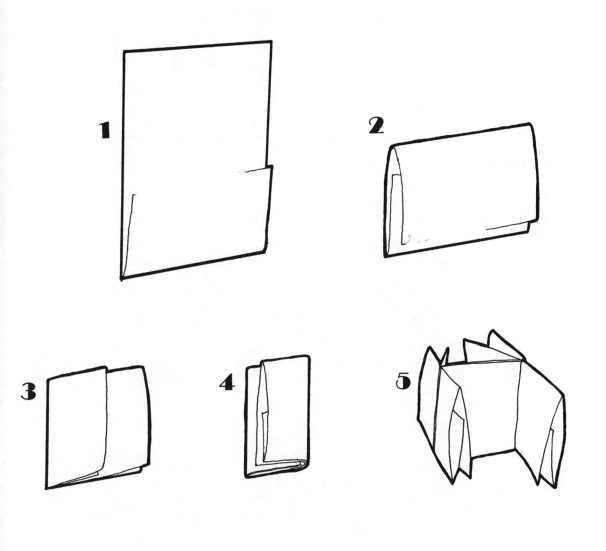

6

(FOLDAWAY, continued)

THE TRICK:

As you follow these instructions, don't fight the natural fold of the creases.

1. Open the large section out flat and keep the middle section in the center of it.
2. Open the middle section out flat.
3. Open the small section out flat, making sure that the smallest flap is at the bottom. Drop a penny onto the center, refold it, starting with that smallest flap and making sure that the largest flap closes last (**6**). Turn it over towards you.
4. Fold up the middle section, starting again with the small flap at the bottom and closing the largest flap last. Turn it over towards you, and leave it in place.
5. Fold the large section around the middle section, still starting with the small flap at the bottom and closing the largest flap last, and then turn it over.
6. Tap the paper twice with your finger.
7. Turn over the paper and open out the large section.
8. Without turning over the middle section, open it up.
9. Turn over the smallest section and open it up to show the coin gone (or you can have a dollar bill there, or an IOU or whatever other flat object you loaded in before you started).
10. Refold the three papers, following Steps 1 through 5.
11. After tapping it twice, again reopen the papers as in Steps 7 to 9 and the coin will have returned.

7

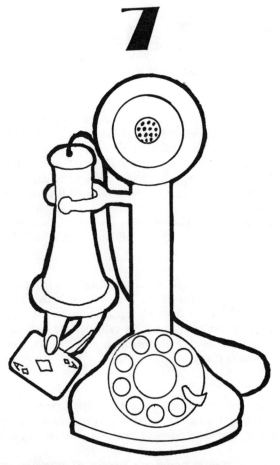

Telephone Trickery

Making a Date

"Here's the best trick you'll see in a month of Sundays...!"

THE ILLUSION:

The next time you're talking to someone on the telephone, and you get to one of those silent spots where neither of you has anything to say, ask your phone friend if he has a calendar in front of him. He then takes a pencil and draws a square around any square block of nine dates, three on each side. When he's done so, you ask him to add up the dates and give you the total. He does and almost immediately you tell him the dates he has boxed.

As a variation, have your friend circle one day in each week in a month on a calendar in front of him. All you do is ask him how many of each day of the week he has circled, and you tell him the total of all the dates.

THE PREPARATION:

For the first effect you need only a calendar in front of you. For the second, you must have your friend use a month with five Wednesdays in it. If the present month doesn't have them, tell him to use one of the months just passed so he doesn't mark up his calendar for this month, and suggest the closest one that has five Wednesdays. Add the total of the five Wednesday dates and you're ready.

THE TRICKS:

When your friend gives you the total in the first trick, divide the total by 9, and this will give you the number of the center square of the nine dates. Starting with that date on your calendar you can name all nine of the dates he boxed.

The second trick is ingeniously simple. After you've convinced your friend to use the month with the five Wednesdays whose total you know, have him circle one day in each of the weeks. Now ask him to tell you how many

			MAY			
SUNDAY	MONDAY	TUESDAY	WEDNESDAY	THURSDAY	FRIDAY	SATURDAY
				1	2	3
4	5	6	7	8	9	10
11	12	13	14	15	16	17
18	19	20	21	22	23	24
25	26	27	28	29	30	31

			JULY			
SUNDAY	MONDAY	TUESDAY	WEDNESDAY	THURSDAY	FRIDAY	SATURDAY
		1	2	3	4	5
6	7	8	9	10	11	12
13	14	15	16	17	18	19
20	21	22	23	24	25	26
27	28	29	30	31		

$126 \div 14$

Wednesday total = 80
$80 + 2 - 3 - 1 + 0 - 2 = 76$

Sundays are circled, how many Mondays, how many Tuesdays, Wednesdays, and so on right through the week. What you are doing is adjusting your Wednesday total with each of his answers:

For each Sunday subtract 3
For each Monday subtract 2
For each Tuesday subtract 1
All the Wednesdays count as zeroes
For each Thursday add 1
For each Friday add 2
For each Saturday add 3

If you adjust your total as he names the days, then as soon as he's told you the number of Saturdays he circled, you can name the total of all the dates circled.

"We must make a date to try this trick again sometime!"

They're in the Book

"Here's a short trick we could even do long distance. . . !"

THE ILLUSION:

While you're talking to a friend on the telephone ask him if he has a full book of matches. If he does, have him tear out any number from 1 to 10. Next he counts the remaining matches, adds the two digits together, and tears out that many more matches. Now he can tear out any number of the remaining matches (the choice is up to him) and hold them in his hand. When he tells you the number of matches in his hand, you are able to tell him how many are still in the packet.

THE TRICK:

By having him add the two digits together you have forced him to finish with 9 matches in the packet. (For example: From a full packet he tears out 7, leaving 13. He adds the digits 1 and 3 and tears out 4 more, leaving 9.) When he tells you the number in his hand, just subtract that number from 9; that's how many are still in the folder.

If this trick doesn't work, you can always claim you've gotten a wrong number.

Phone-y Numbers

"Alexander Graham Bell could've done this trick, if he'd been smart enough to invent the phone book...!"

THE ILLUSION:

> While talking to a friend on the telephone you invite him to do a trick with you. He writes down any three-digit number, adds a zero on the end, and then subtracts his original number. He adds all the digits in the answer and then turns to that page in his telephone book. Miles away you're able to tell him the first name on that page.

THE TRICK:

> Have a copy of the same telephone book handy when you ask your friend to do a trick with you. No matter what number he starts with, he will always arrive at the number 9.
> For example, he writes down any three-digit number (137)
> He adds a zero on the end (1370)
> He subtracts his original number (1370 – 137 = 1233)
> He adds all the digits until he has only a one-digit number (1 + 2 + 3 + 3 = 9)
> He turns to that page and looks at the first name

While he's doing his computations, you calmly turn to page 9 so that when he turns to that page, you already know the name.

> If he asks you to do it again, you can—but differently. This time ask him to: Write down any three-digit number (137)
> Reverse it and subtract the smaller from the larger (731 – 137 = 594)
> Reverse the answer and add the two together (594 + 495 = 1089)

Add all the digits together and turn to that page. This time, no matter which number he starts with, he will finish with 18.

> "I learned that trick from an old friend . . . Ma Bell!"

Teletrick

"I promise—this'll be the most amazing trick you ever didn't see...!"

THE ILLUSION:

When you're talking to a friend on the phone ask him to dig up a deck of cards. You then ask him to cut the deck in three piles, select one of them, and put the other cards aside. He then cuts the cards he retained in three new piles, removes a card from one of them, memorizes it, replaces it, and reassembles the piles. Finally, you ask him to name the cards as he deals them out. When he has finished, you tell him the name of the card he memorized.

THE TRICK:

Before talking to your friend prepare a sheet of paper with the numbers 1 to 24 in a column. Have your friend shuffle the cards and then cut them into three fairly equal piles. Next he picks up any one of the three piles and discards the other two. Using the cards in his selected pile, he deals the cards out into three equal packets, discarding any odd cards left over. He now removes any card from the center of any of the three piles, looks at the card, memorizes it, and replaces it on top of its pile. Any one of the other piles goes on top of this pile, and all of these cards are dropped on the remaining pile. Ask him to name the cards as he deals them from the top face up onto the table. As soon as he's named the first card, stop him and say, "Oh, did you cut the cards?" He'll say no, so tell him to return that card to the top and cut the deck. While he's doing this you write down the name of the card he called off to one side of your column.

Then, as he is naming the cards, you check off each of the numbers in the column in front of you in sequence. (As he names the first card, you check off #1; as he names the second card, you check off #2.) As soon as he names the card he named the first time (the one you wrote down) you circle that number. From this point on, you write down the names of the third,

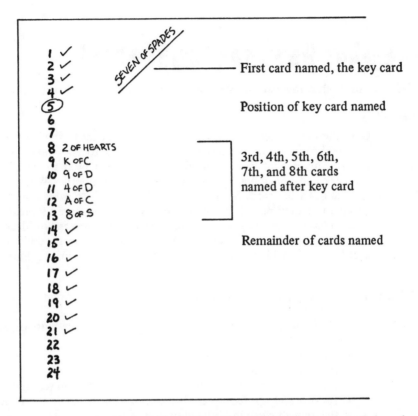

1 ✓
2 ✓
3 ✓
4 ✓
⑤
6
7
8 2 OF HEARTS
9 K OF C
10 9 OF D
11 4 OF D
12 A OF C
13 8 OF S
14 ✓
15 ✓
16 ✓
17 ✓
18 ✓
19 ✓
20 ✓
21 ✓
22
23
24

SEVEN OF SPADES

———— First card named, the key card

Position of key card named

3rd, 4th, 5th, 6th,
7th, and 8th cards
named after key card

Remainder of cards named

fourth, fifth, sixth, seventh, and eighth cards after the one you circled, and then go back to checking off the rest of the numbers. As soon as he stops naming cards you will know how many cards are in the pile. Divide that number by three, and his memorized card is that far down from your circle. For example, if he has named 21 cards then there were 7 cards in each of the three piles, and his memorized card is the seventh one after your circle.

"You know how I did that trick? I did it with mirrors."

Magic Impossible!

"Hello, Mr. Phelps. Follow my instructions exactly and I won't self-destruct. . . !"

THE ILLUSION:

Over the phone you ask someone to get a deck of cards, shuffle the deck, and to quietly remove any number of cards from 1 to 10, count them and put them in his pocket. Now using that same number he is to count down into the deck and remember the card that lies at that number. When he has done that he deals the cards faceup one at a time and is to name only their colors to you, not their names. Finally, you stop him and have him reassemble the deck. You ask him only whether his selected card was red or black. When he answers, you think for a moment and then tell him how far down to count in the deck to find his memorized card. He follows your instructions, and there it is.

THE TRICK: The trick is practically automatic—all you have to do is remember where you stopped him.

1. He counts off any number from 1 to 10 and puts those cards in his pocket.
2. Using the same number, he looks at the card at that number from the top of the deck.
3. He deals cards faceup, naming their color, until you tell him to stop.
4. He turns all the faceup cards facedown on the table and then drops the undealt cards in his hand on top of them.

The key is that as he was naming the colors of the cards, you were counting them. When you get to between 15 and 20, you stop him and have him reassemble the deck (Step 4). Now, from 52, mentally subtract the number at which you stopped him. Tell him to deal off that many cards one at a time from the top facedown. When he's done that, tell him to turn over the last card dealt. It's his memorized card. Voila!

"Guess how this trick was done. Your deck was bugged!"

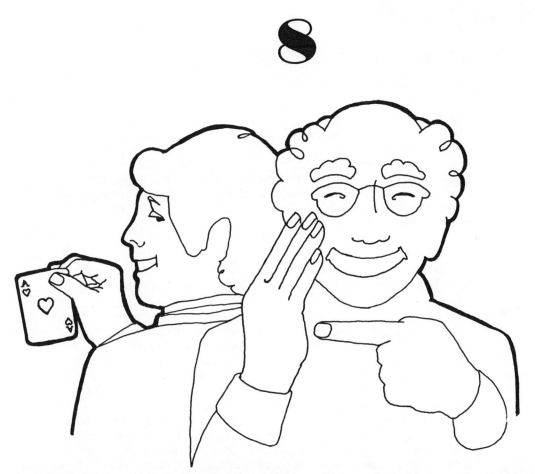

When Friends Get Together

You Don't Have to be Crazy

"Here's a trick I learned from the Invisible Man. . . !"

THE ILLUSION:

You remove a make-believe deck of cards from your pocket, have someone pretend to shuffle the pack and deal one card to each person in the crowd. Following your instructions, each "cardholder" does a quick computation based on the value of the card he has supposedly been given, tells you the imaginary sum of the computation and returns his card to the invisible deck. You run through the imaginary cards and put a selected card on the table, correctly naming it as you do so.

THE PREPARATION:

This is the ideal trick for those occasions when you are asked to do a little something and you have nothing at hand—except your imagination!

THE TRICK:

Remove the nonexistent cards from your pocket, pantomime taking them out of the case, and hand the "deck" to a woman for shuffling. In the middle of the first shuffle tell her she doesn't have to be nervous, and to please pick up the card she just dropped on the floor. Have her deal one card each to the people closest to her, because *you* don't want to be accused of sleight-of-hand. They "remember" their cards and return them to the deck.

Now, you must figure out what each card is. First of all, ask each person to think of just the number of his or her card. Face cards are to be a continuation of the numbering; that is, Jack is 11, the Queen 12, and the King 13. Next, ask them to double the number of the card. Add one to it. That number is multiplied by 5. Now they consider the suit by adding its value; 6 for a Club, 7 for Hearts, 8 for any Spade, and 9 if it's a Diamond. [To remember the order of the suits just think of the word "CHaSeD," to remind you of Clubs, Hearts, Spades, and Diamonds.

You pick up the imaginary deck and ask for the first selector's total. When it's given to you, figure out the suit. This is done by using the last digit of the answer; if it's a 1, the card is a Club, a 2 means a Heart, 3 is a Spade, and a 4 denotes Diamonds. If the answer isn't one of these digits, tell the person they made a mistake and to check the arithmetic. Now to find the number of the card, you use the first digit of the answer. Subtract 1 from that first digit and there is your number.

Let's say someone gives you the total of 82. The 2 means it's a Heart, and by subtracting 1 from the 8 we arrive at the selected card—the Seven of Hearts. So you go through the motions of removing an invisible card from the "deck," which you show to the person and say, "There it is, the Seven of Hearts. Right?" Be sure to have him acknowledge that that is indeed his card! If the number is 100 or more, use the last digit to determine the suit and take away 1 from the first two digits to determine the number.

"What's the sound of invisible hands clapping?"

Cut and Uncut

"I've heard of scissors so sharp that you can hardly see where they've cut . . ."

THE ILLUSION:

A length of string is threaded through a soda straw until the straw is in the center of the string. The straw is then doubled over and cut in half. However, when the string is pulled out, it's been restored, and is none the worse for wear!

THE PREPARATION:

Ahead of time, put a two-inch slit along the straw at the center with a razor blade (1). Be sure to handle the straw by the ends so that the slit stays closed and unnoticed. You will need a length of thin kite or package string at least fifteen inches long.

THE TRICK:

Openly push the string through the straw until there is string hanging out each end. Bend the straw in half so that the slit is to the inside of the fold. Grip the straw in the left fist and pull on the two ends of the string with your right hand. This will pull the string out of the center of the straw and through the slit so it is an inch below the fold. Pick up the scissors, put the lower blade through the fold of the straw, but above the string, and cut (2). Take the lower ends of the straw in the right fingers and pull the string and straw down into the left fist until they stick out the bottom. Lift one end up all the way between your thumb and index finger so you have an end of straw sticking out each side of your left fist (3). Wave the scissors over your left hand and pull out the string to show it "restored."

"I'm working my way up to sawing a woman in half."

1

2

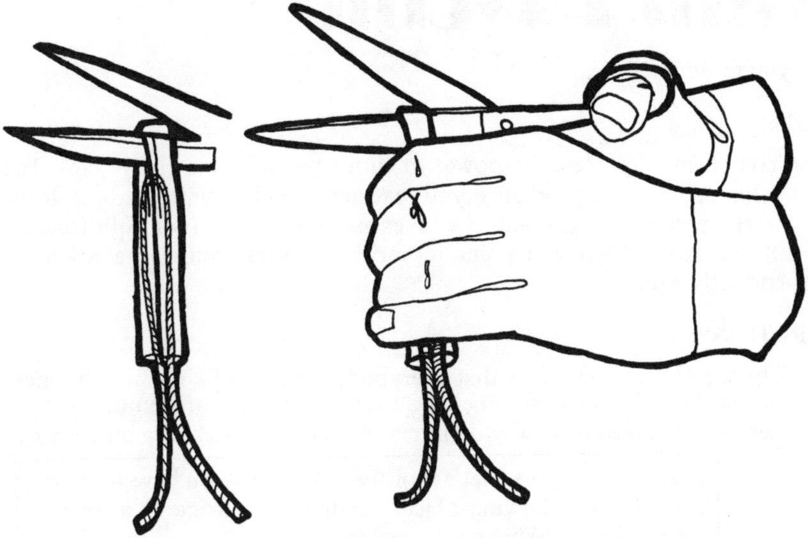

3

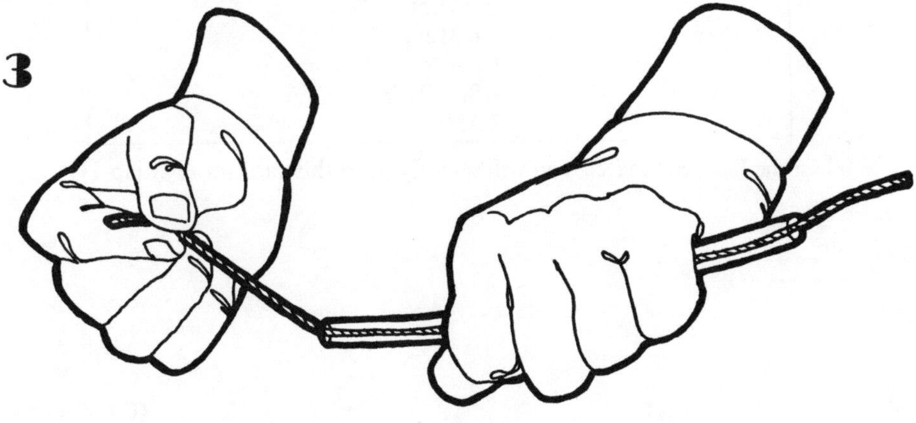

Instant Psychic

"I know what you're thinking . . ."

THE ILLUSION:

You claim to possess the power to turn anyone into a clairvoyant. Taking a volunteer from the audience you seat her in a chair with her back to the rest of the party. You gaze into her eyes and lay the palms of both hands on top of her head. Then you point to various objects around the room and she correctly names them.

THE PREPARATION:

The secret of this trick is that everybody wants to be in show business. The person brought forward to help you is not a confederate—until you sit him or her down! Ahead of time you have written on the back of a business card:

> Be a good sport. Let's fool the others. All you have to do is name the following objects in this order—one at a time— when I say, "What am I touching now?"
>
> WATCH
> TABLE
> CHAIR
> ASHTRAY
> LAMP

When she has been seated you will secretly drop this card into her lap **(1)**

(Continued)

1

THE TRICK:

Explain to your audience that mindreading is a latent potential in every person and merely needs the proper development. Have the group pick someone to help you and, as you seat her, drop the card into her lap with the writing side up. You gaze into her eyes, and then place both hands on top of her head and gently bend it downwards so she can see and read the card in her lap (2).

Talk about establishing rapport between two minds, your last sentence as you tell her you're going to make her a mindreader is, "Do you understand?" Look into both eyes as you ask this, and you will know by the answer that, indeed, the trick will work. Walk around the room looking as though you don't know which object to try first. Finally point to someone's watch and ask "What am I touching?" (3). Look for the other items on the list and have them identified one at a time. Finally lead the applause for your helper and be sure to say "Thank you."

If you happen to have a skeptic in the audience who gives you a hard time as you are performing, ask that person to help you next. This time don't supply the secret cue card but do go through all the other buildup with the eyes and hands. Then, after you have asked for the identification of the first object, agree with whatever answer the skeptic gives you. Wink at the audience so they understand what is going to happen, and from then on, no matter what object is named by the heckler, you all agree that he has guessed correctly. This is guaranteed fun, as the skeptic won't be able to figure out how he's doing it! Just lucky, I guess!

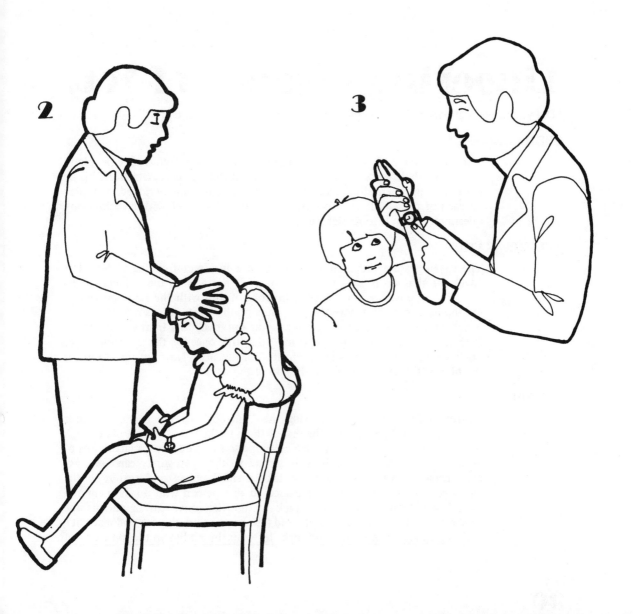

Lingering Essence of You

"Did you know that personal objects pick up more than just fingerprints. . . ?"

THE ILLUSION:

You turn your back so that you can't see, and instruct four or five people to reach into their pockets and remove small objects. Each person seals his or her object in an envelope and the envelopes are thoroughly mixed. You pick up each of the envelopes, open it, gaze at the object, and, without asking any questions, return it to its rightful owner!

THE PREPARATION:

The envelopes are prepared ahead of time with a secret coding system. Use envelopes that do not have glue running all the way to the corners on the flap. Put an envelope on the table in front of you with the flap uppermost. On the back next to where the glue ends on the right, put a small dot with a pencil (1). On the second envelope you put two dots in the same place. Prepare four envelopes like this, and on a fifth one, for the convenience of quick recognition, use a small line instead of five dots. Now put the envelopes in order, with the "one-dot" on the top of the stack.

THE TRICK:

Distribute the envelopes by giving the "one-dot" to the person on your extreme left and passing out the rest of them to the right. If there are enough people, skip a person between each envelope so that you cover a larger area of your audience. After your back is turned so that you surely can't see, ask each person with an envelope to take a small object and seal it in the envelope. All the envelopes are passed to one person who mixes them and then hands them to you. You pick up the first one, tear or cut off the smallest possible sliver at the right end (the same end with your coding on it), and as <u>you are opening the envelope, let your thumb lift up the loose end of</u>

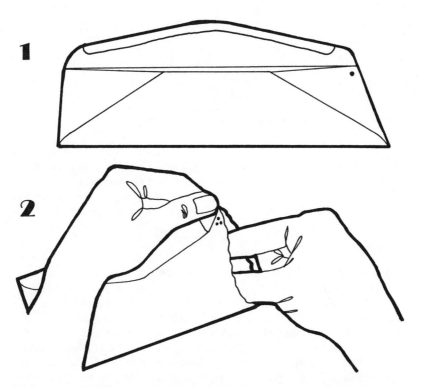

1

2

the flap so that you can see your coding dots **(2)**. If it is three dots then you know the object came from the third person to whom you gave an envelope, and you mentally count people from left to right until you know who that is.

Now try to find some way to associate the object with the person; is the item the same color as her eyes, does it have an artistic flair like the individual, does it show the intelligence of the person? Or, if nothing occurs to you, just "gather in the personal emanations of the psychic aura" and return it. The main thing to remember is to flatter each owner before you identify him. Each time you open an envelope, you will know who you are going to talk about, so make it interesting!

"Isn't it wonderful how we make lasting impressions!"

Easy On, Easy Off

"Do you ever have trouble with things slipping through your fingers. . . ?"

THE ILLUSION:

> Someone threads a cord through a borrowed finger ring, and you tie a knot around it. Two handkerchiefs also are knotted around the cord and someone holds each end. A quick gesture and the captive ring magically dissolves the knot and comes off into your hand—leaving the two handkerchiefs still tied to the cord.

THE PREPARATION:

> It's all in the way you tie the knot. Practice this a few times by taking a piece of cord or light rope about a yard long and running it through one of your rings. Slide the ring to the center and place your hands about six inches on each side of it; the left hand with the cupped palm upwards, and the right hand with your knuckles upwards (1). Now turn the fingers of each fist in until the fingernails of each hand are opposite each other, then straighten out the first two fingers of each hand. Move your hands in to the center so those fingers can grip the rope in the opposite hand. The left fingers go inside the right hand and grip the rope below the right thumb. The right two fingers go behind the left hand and grip the rope just above the left thumb (2). Gripping the rope tightly with those two fingers, open the other fingers on each hand and separate the two hands. Keep pulling until you have formed a tight bowknot with loops about four or five inches long, with your ring right in the center. Holding each loop between each pair of fingers turn your hands until the index fingers are uppermost. Reaching down through the left loop with the left thumb and index finger, pull the rope all the way up through the loop. Move your right thumb under its loop to help turn the loop away from you, one half-turn, and then pull its rope up through the loop (3). Run the left end of the cord through the ring. Pull on the ends of the cord and the

(Continued)

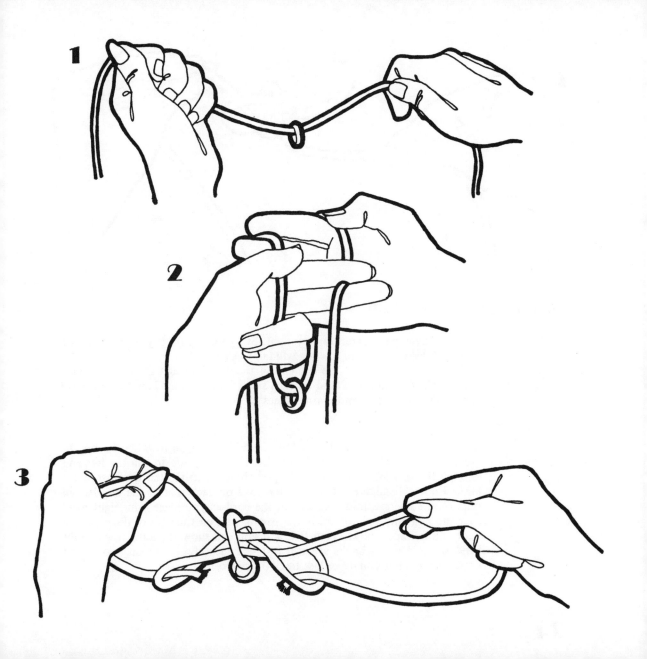

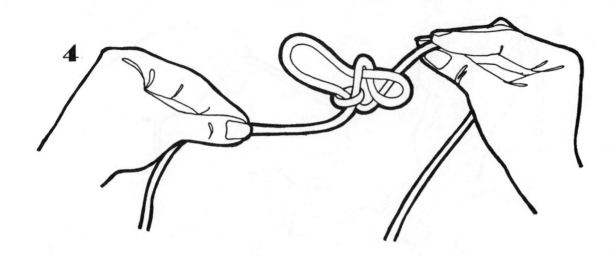

4

(EASY ON, EASY OFF, continued)

knot will become apparently very tight. Stop pulling, for if you continue the knot will disintegrate and the ring will fall free **(4)**.

If, after you have put the left end of the cord through the ring, you tie a handkerchief around the cord on each side of the ring, the handkerchiefs will remain on the cord when the ring comes off.

THE TRICK:

Give someone the cord and have him thread his ring on it. Slide the ring to the center and make your special bowknot, making sure to run the left end through the ring after tying it. Then pull the cord to tighten the bow into a knot. Knot a handkerchief around the cord on each side of the imprisoned ring. Have someone hold each end of the cord as you place your right hand over the ring and its knot. Have the person pull on the ends of the cord, the knot will fall apart inside your fist, and you can show the loose ring in your hand while the two hanks are still fastened securely. Knots may come and knots may go, but you *never* lose track of jewelry!

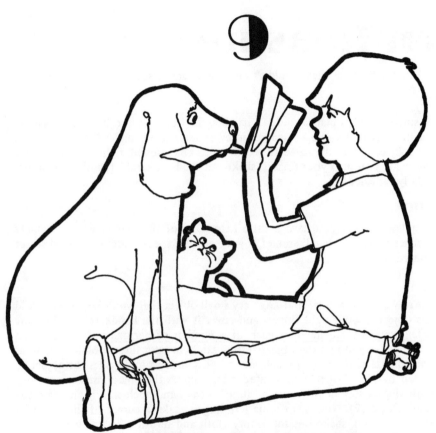

The Fun of
Sharing the Secret

Stolen Treasure

"Does anyone have a small object they wouldn't miss for a year or so. . . ?"

THE ILLUSION:

A small object is placed under a handkerchief and, to preclude any cheating on the part of the sneaky magician, everyone reaches under the cloth to feel the object. They all agree it is still solid and present right up to the last moment. You snap your fingers, shake out the handkerchief, and the item has totally vanished!

THE PREPARATION:

Needless to say, you have a little help. One of the people who obligingly reaches under the handkerchief is your equally sneaky sticky-fingered secret confederate.

THE TRICK:

Borrow a handkerchief and any very small object that won't be missed! Hold the object in your right fingers and cover it with the handkerchief (1). Now offer your covered hand to each of a number of persons so they each can reach under and feel the object resting safely in your fingers. Make sure your confederate is the last to reach in, and all you have to do is let the object be stolen by him. When your confederate removes the object, make sure your right fingers stay in the same position so the handkerchief will maintain the same shape (2). Now snap your left fingers, take a corner of the hanky in your left hand, shake out the empty cloth and return it to its owner. As for the small object that has disappeared . . . the tooth fairy always wanted one of those!

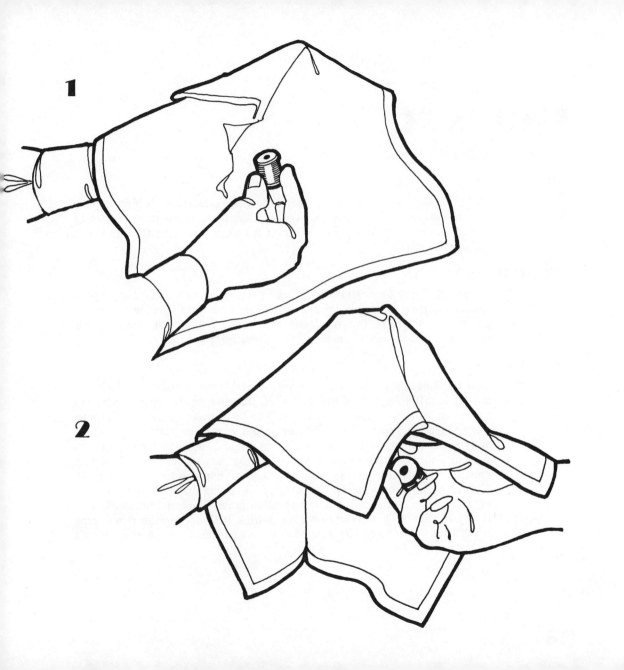

1

2

That's It

"You may not believe this, but she and I think as one. . . !"

THE ILLUSION:

While you are guarded in another room, the group selects some object in plain view of everyone. You return and various things around the room are named one after another. When the right object is named you instantly verify it as the selected one!

THE PREPARATION:

Once again your confederate either can be a secret or openly can be your special assistant. How does your assistant know when to indicate the proper object? He doesn't! The secret of this very baffling and unfathomable mystery is that you are the one to do the signaling. Read on!

THE TRICK:

You come back into the room and your friend starts naming or pointing to objects in different parts of the room (1). Four, five, or six objects are named and when you want the selected object to be named you merely do something to change your position; fold or unfold your arms, shift one foot, put your hands behind you, or any other natural and subtle movement (2). As soon as your confederate sees you do this, the next object he or she names must be the selected one. As soon as it is, you name it as the group's choice.

Just this once, let yourself be pressured into doing the same trick twice, or even three times, as the fun and frustration grow. The insidious subtlety of this particular while-I'm-out-of-the-room trick is that <u>everyone is watching and listening to your assistant</u>, waiting for a signal that will never come. It's all in knowing how.

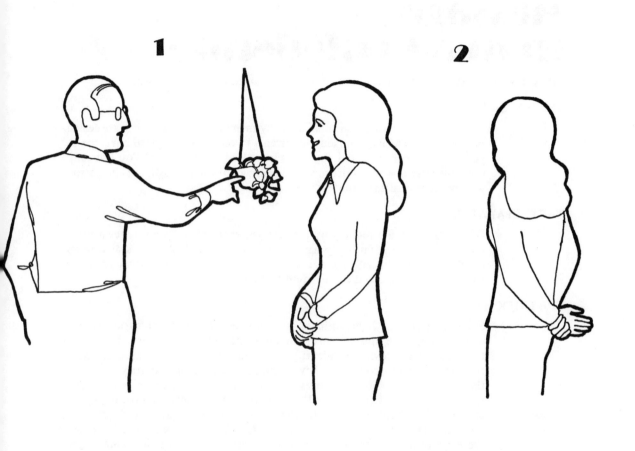

Message from a Confederate

"Do you know certain people can smell color, see music, or hear the written word...?"

THE ILLUSION:

Short messages, written on small cards by members of the audience are sealed in envelopes, which are mixed and given to you. You hold each envelope to your ear, concentrate, and say what is written on the inside. You not only open the envelope and confirm your "reading" of the message, but the person who wrote it verifies it, too!

THE PREPARATION:

Once more you are rescued by a secret assistant. Your friend writes a short message which was mutually agreed upon beforehand. As it is sealed in its envelope, your assistant makes a strong dent in one corner of that envelope with his thumbnail, so it can be identified later (1).

THE TRICK:

Small invitation cards or business cards are good to use for this trick as they will all look alike and are small enough so people won't automatically fold them and thus provide an identifying factor later. When the messages have been written and sealed away, have them collected and mixed. As you receive the envelopes and look them over, find the one with the nail nick and shuffle it to the bottom of the stack (2). Take any of the others and hold it to your ear. After due deliberation recite the prearranged message. Now, to confirm your divination you open the envelope. Quickly memorize what is written there as your confederate acknowledges the first message as being his or hers . . . and correct.

When you "listen" to the second envelope, you repeat the message you just memorized. This way you are one message ahead of your audience all the way through the stack. Your confederate's envelope is the last to be picked

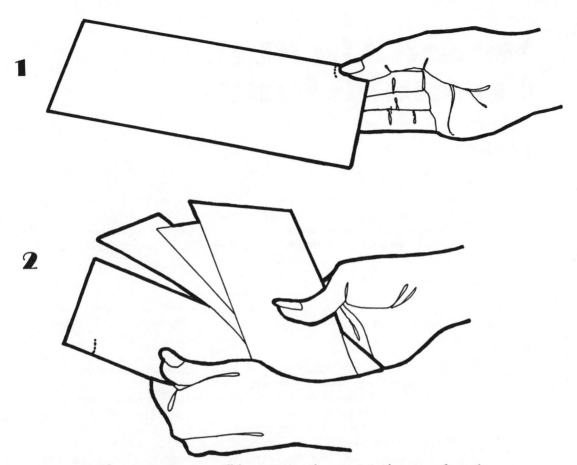

up and, once again, you will be repeating the memorized message from the previous envelope.

Remember, each time you are memorizing the real message from inside the envelope, act as though you are merely confirming what you just said. <u>Smile, nod your head in agreement, and once in a while you can even say, "Right!"</u> And on good nights you might even pick up radio messages from Pittsburgh.

We Are About to Commit a Crime

"I'll bet Sherlock Holmes would have been a great magician . . ."

THE ILLUSION:

While you are out of the room someone picks up some small object and, with great melodrama, uses it as a "weapon" to pretend to "murder" one of the other people in the party. Now the "murderer" conceals the "weapon" on one of the innocent bystanders and takes a seat to "hide out." You, the super sleuth, come back into the room and, without asking any questions, find the weapon, identify the victim, and correctly accuse the perpetrator of the foul deed!

THE PREPARATION:

One of the innocent bystanders is your secret confederate. All your friend has to do is to duplicate the positions of the various characters in a certain order.

THE TRICK:

You set the stage by telling the group that a crime is about to be committed. Then you retire to another room with someone to act as a guard to keep you from peeking. While you are gone the murder weapon is picked, pointed at a victim, hidden on another person, and the murderer retires to the anonymity of the crowd. The more ludicrous the murder weapon, the greater the fun. (Being shot by a key or stabbed by a pillow is real melodrama!) As you are being brought back into the room, your confederate assumes the same posture as the murderer; placement of feet and hands, and general attitude. Ten seconds later your confederate changes position to match that of the victim. Another ten seconds and the duplication is now of the person hiding the weapon, and a final shift of a hand indicates where on that person the weapon can be found. All this is done as you wander about the room <u>looking into people's faces and mumbling to yourself</u> like any good deductive detec-

tive. Finally, when you have all the information, you produce the weapon, identify the victim, and accuse the murderer. The more dramatic you make the various steps, the greater the fun, and the more amazing your discoveries. I wonder if Columbo started like this?

The Secret of Yeah-Yep-Yes

"Of course, I believe in ESP ... doesn't everyone...?"

THE ILLUSION:

You, being the very fair person you are, turn your back while each of five or six people selects cards from a deck. While your back is still turned you are able to identify first the color, then the suit, and finally the number of each card!

THE PREPARATION:

This simple code has been used by professional magicians for decades. The person who shares the code with you either can be used secretly or can be openly acknowledged as working with you, at your discretion. You each have memorized a very simple way to transmit the names of playing cards using only three simple words. Your friend is the one who points to each card and asks you to identify it. First of all, here is the code:

Clubs—1 word   Hearts—2 words   Spades—3 words   Diamonds—4 or more words

(The way to remember the sequence: Clubs, Hearts, Spades, Diamonds, is to think of the word CHaSeD.)

	Yeah	Yep	Yes	(silence)
Yeah	Ace	5	9	
Yep	2	6	10	
Yes	3	7	Jack	
(silence)	4	8	Queen	King

THE TRICK:

You turn your back and explain to the group that each person who removed a card from the deck is to place it faceup on the table. Your friend will then point to any of the cards and ask you to identify it. Your confederate first has to transmit the suit of the selected card (for example, the Nine of Hearts). He or she must say a sentence containing the right number of words (for the Nine of Hearts it must be two words; something like, "Ready, John?"). Now you know the suit but you need more information, so you make a statement about just the color ("I believe that is a red card."). Your assistant can now code to you the proper column containing the value of the card. (He would say "Yes," meaning it is in the third column, containing the 9, 10, Jack, and Queen.) At this point you name the suit ("That's a Heart, isn't it?"). In response, your helpful friend codes to you the position of the selected card in that column by uttering the proper cue word ("Yeah," being the first cue word means it is the first card in the appropriate column). You can now name the card ("I'm positive I see the Nine of Hearts, is that correct?"). The reply to this then codes the suit of the next card ("Right!" meaning the next card is a Club).

If the selected card is a King, then both the cues for the value are silence itself, or "Uh huh," replaced sometimes with "Mm hmm."

Remember, to figure out the value of the card, first think down, and then across. Another example: Queen of Spades.

HE: Name the card (3 words, cueing "Spade")

YOU: Is it a black card?

HE: Yes. (Indicating that you must mentally run down the third column, 9, 10, Jack, Queen.)

YOU: Is it a Spade?

HE: Uh huh. (Signaling that you should think across the SILENT row to the third column.)

YOU: It's the Queen of Spades.

10

Take a Card...

The Card that Counts

"Have you ever seen a deck of cards do a trick by itself. . . ?"

THE ILLUSION:

Someone selects a card from the pack, memorizes it, and places it on top of the deck. The deck is cut and spread on the table, and there is a card faceup in the center. The person who has selected it immediately tells you it's not his card, and you agree. However, you say, just count the number of spots on the reversed card and count down that many cards. He does so, and there is his selected card, right where the deck said it would be!

THE PREPARATION:

Beforehand you have secretly reversed a card at the bottom of the deck. Now place below that card a number of cards equal to one less than its value **(1)**. For example, if you reversed an 8 you would then put seven cards below it. All of these cards are facing the same direction as the rest of the deck; your indicator card is the only reversed one.

THE TRICK:

Run the cards from hand to hand, and have one card selected. Just make sure you don't go too close to the bottom and expose the reversed card. Put the deck on the table and have the card returned to the top. Then have your selector cut the deck and square it neatly. Snap your fingers over the cards and spread them across the table. There is your indicator card faceup in the center **(2)**.

Remove all the cards above the indicator card and push it toward the person who selected a card. He counts the spots on the indicator, counts down that far in the remainder of the deck, turns over the card at that number, and there is his card. Thank you, cards.

1

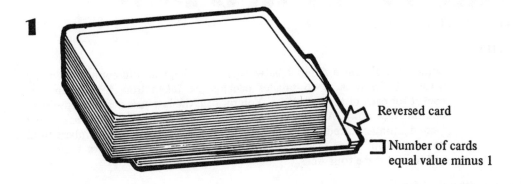

Reversed card

Number of cards
equal value minus 1

2

That's Four in a Row

"This deck really has your number. . . !"

THE ILLUSION:

Someone calls out a number between 10 and 20, and you count that many cards off the deck. Two smaller packets are taken from that group, one packet for each of the two digits. You pick up the last card dealt and put it to one side face down. All the cards are gathered up, replaced on the deck, and a second number asked for. You repeat the process with new numbers until you have four cards face down in a row. Have an onlooker turn them over and there are the four Aces.

THE PREPARATION:

You have put the four Aces on top of the pack with nine cards on top of them (**1**).

The rest is automatic.

THE TRICK:

Ask for any number between 10 and 20. Let's say someone calls out 15. Count that many cards into a pile in front of you and set the deck aside (**2**). Pick up the 15 cards and tell your audience that a 15 is made of a one (deal a single card slightly to your left) and a five [deal five cards just to the right of the single one (**3**)]. Remove the last card you dealt and put it to one side face down; it is an Ace but you don't show it (**4**). Drop the cards remaining in your hand on top of the remainder of the right-hand pile, place all of those cards on the single card to the left, and put all of them back on top of the deck.

Ask for another number from 10 to 20, and repeat the process by counting off that many cards and then making two smaller piles equal to the two digits of the number. The last card dealt is always placed to one side. When you have all four Aces together, turn them over. That'll be four Aces over easy.

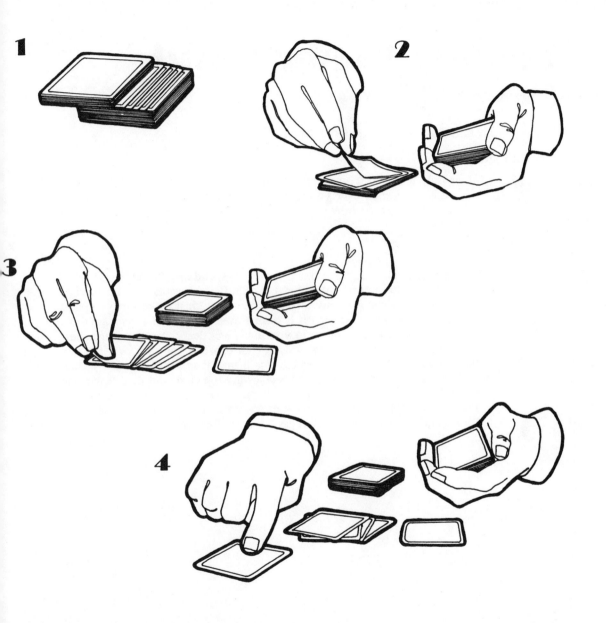

Perfect Poker Hand Every Time

"I'm practicing until I can do this with a full deck . . ."

THE ILLUSION:

Using only ten cards, you deal poker hands to a spectator and yourself. When the cards are turned over you have won the hand. You keep repeating the action and, no matter how much you shuffle the cards, you always have the better hand.

THE TRICK:

You use three Sevens, three Tens, three Kings, and any Ace except the Ace of Spades, which is too noticeable (1). Shuffle the cards face up in your hands to show there isn't any setting of the cards. Just make sure you place the Ace so that when the packet is turned over, it will be the first card dealt (2). Turn the cards face down in your hand and deal out two poker hands, giving your opponent the first card, of course. When you turn over the two hands you will find your poker hand is higher than his (3). Gather up the cards, making sure the Ace again becomes the top card, and mix them some more, keeping the Ace on top. Deal, and once more you'll win. Three times is the most you should do the trick; it proves your point but isn't enough times for anyone to figure it out. Las Vegas was never like this.

1

2

3

Ace on the Bottom

"Do you remember how to count from 1 to 10...?"

THE ILLUSION:

One of the members of your audience selects a card from the center of the deck, memorizes it, and cuts it back into the pack. The bottom card, where she cut the pack, is used as an indicator card; using its value she counts down that far into the cards, turns over the next card, and there is her card looking at her!

THE PREPARATION:

You must have a secret setup on the bottom of the deck. Remove the Ace through 10 of any one suit and set them in reverse order. That is, the Ace is the bottom card and the 10 is the top card of the packet when the cards are face down. Put this packet on the bottom of the deck (1).

THE TRICK:

Put the deck in front of someone and ask for a card to be removed from the center. After it has been noted it is dropped on top of the deck, and the deck is cut. Pick up the pack and, as you put it in front of a second spectator, turn it face up. Have him cut the deck and complete the cut. What you want is for him to cut the pack within your secret setup—the run from Ace to 10. If the new card on the face of the deck is one of your suit, then you're ready to finish the trick. If the new card is a face card of your suit or is from some other suit, the deck has to be cut some more until you do get one of your cards face up. As soon as you do, have the second spectator name the value of that card out loud (2). Then pick up the deck and give it back to the person who originally selected the card, turning it rightside up as you do so. She now counts off cards from the top of the deck to equal the value of the indicator card and puts the last card dealt face down to one side. Pick up the deck and

114

ask her to name her selected card out loud. After she's named her card, tell her to turn over the single card (it's hers). At the same time you pick up the remaining cards on the table and casually mix the two packets together to destroy your run of setup cards. For an honest person, that was a sneaky thing for you to do.

With the Help of Si Stebbins

"Can you believe I don't do this for a living. . . !"

THE ILLUSION:

You are able to do three card tricks that are utterly inexplicable and you accomplish them without sleight of hand or tedious practice.

THE PREPARATION:

You are about to learn how to stack a deck and perform tricks actually used by professional magicians. First of all, how to set up the deck.

Separate the cards by suits into four face-up piles with each pile in correct order, Ace to King with the King looking right at you. Put the piles in order from left to right as Clubs, Hearts, Spades, and Diamonds. Leave the packet with King of Clubs untouched. Cut ten cards from the face of the packet of Hearts, put them on bottom of Heart pack so that the pack now has the Three of Hearts on top. Cut seven cards from packet of Spades and put them on bottom of that pack. You now have a Six of Spades on top. Cut four cards from packet of Diamonds, so that the Nine of Diamonds is facing you (1). Now pick up the King of Clubs and put it, still face up, in your left hand. Go to the second pile, pick up the Three of Hearts and put it face up on top of the King in your hand (2). Then add the Six of Spades and the Nine of Diamonds from the third and fourth piles. Now pick up the Queen of Clubs and keep picking up cards from the four piles until the entire deck is face up in your left hand. Finally, turn the entire deck face down. You have just set the deck in an order magicians call "Si Stebbins."

Run through the deck and you'll find that the suits run Clubs, Hearts, Spades, and Diamonds, and keep repeating that order all the way down through the deck. Also, by adding 3 to any card and progressing to the next suit in order, you will know the name of the following card. For example, if

(Continued)

1

2

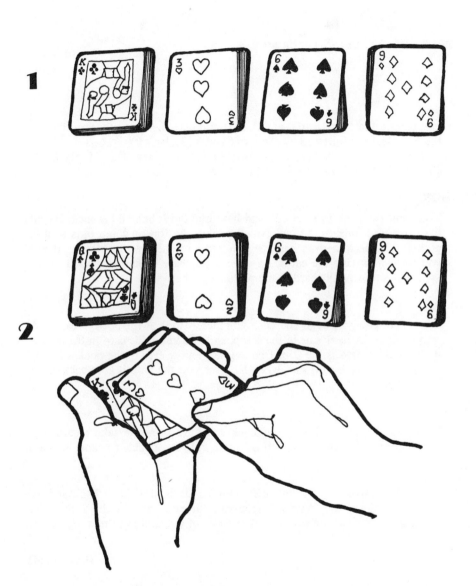

you choose the 5 of Hearts, add 3 to it and take the next suit, you find that the 5 of Hearts is followed by the 8 of Spades (3). Isn't it?

Just remember, in between tricks just cut the pack—DON'T SHUFFLE and DON'T CUT CARDS FROM THE CENTER.

FIRST ILLUSION:

You hand the deck to someone and have him put it behind his back. He cuts the cards and finishes the cut. Now he takes the top card and puts it in his pocket. The deck is given back to you and you quickly run through it as if you are memorizing the cards. As soon as you have looked at the last card of the pack you name the card in the person's pocket.

THE TRICK:

As you are going through the deck you merely look at the bottom card. Add 3 to it, take the next suit in the setup, and you know the card in the pocket. If the bottom card is the 2 of Diamonds, then the card in the pocket is the 5 of Clubs (4). Make sure that when he gives you the card it goes back on top of the pack.

SECOND ILLUSION:

You hold the deck behind your back and have someone take a card from anywhere in the pack. Without turning around you are able to name her card.

THE TRICK:

Spread the cards slightly between your hands behind your back and ask anyone to take a card. As she is removing the card, separate the deck at that point. Bring the two halves around in front of you and put them together so

(Continued)

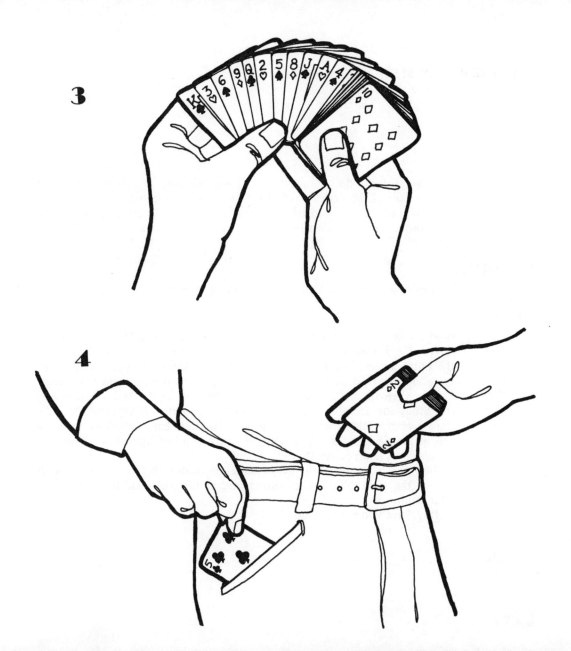

3

4

you have cut the deck where the card was removed (5). Now peek at the bottom card of the deck (which was just above the selected card when it was removed), add 3 to it and take the next suit. Name the selected card. Once again make sure that when she gives you the card it goes back on top of the pack.

THIRD ILLUSION:

Someone cuts the deck. You name a card and its position in the deck.

THE TRICK:

Hold the deck in your left hand and have someone cut it. Make sure it is cut in your hand. Complete the cut, and as you set the deck on the table, peek at the bottom card. This time you don't add 3 to the value, you use the same value and the next suit in your setup. Say the bottom card was the Jack of Spades, then the card you are going to name will be the Jack of Diamonds (6). Study the deck for a moment as though you are making mental calculations (which is fairly true!) and then say, "The thirteenth card down from the top of the deck is the . . ." naming the card you just figured out. Someone counts down and you are absolutely right.

Just remember, you will always name the thirteenth card from the top. It will be the same value as the bottom card of the pack, and the next suit in your setup.

Boy, have you gotten good.

5

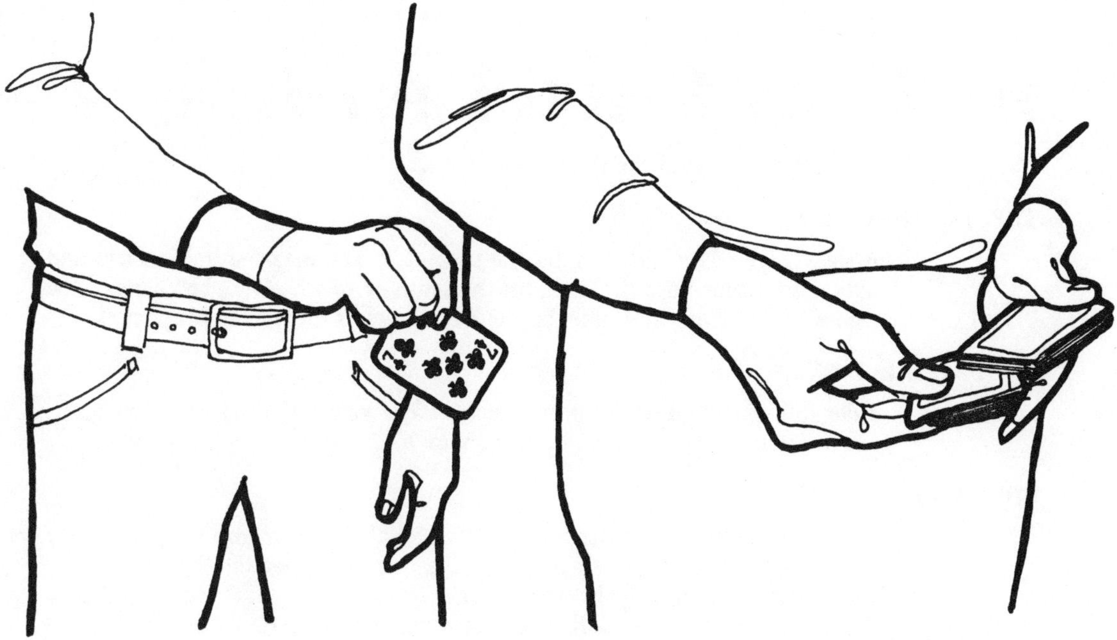

6

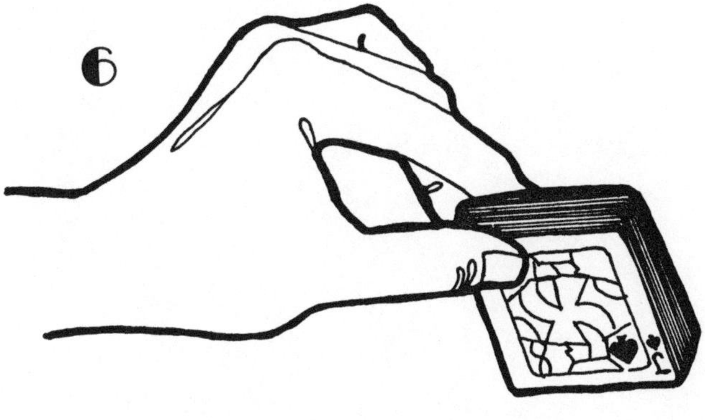

Instant Card Reading

"You can't tell, but I have an eye at the end of my finger. . . !"

THE ILLUSION:

A pack of cards is shuffled by the spectator. The magician takes them and puts them in his pocket. Then, by the sense of touch alone, he calls out the names of cards, one at a time, before he withdraws them from his pocket.

THE PREPARATION:

Take five or six cards from the deck before giving them to the spectator, memorize their sequence, and put them in your pocket.

THE TRICK:

Ask the spectator to shuffle the deck thoroughly and give you the deck. Place the cards in your pocket so that they are directly under the five or six cards which you have already in your pocket. Reach into your pocket and take them out one at a time, calling out their names before you take them out and show them. If you don't stop after six, your fingers are on their own.

11

Crafty Magic

"The Old Coin-in-the-Corner Trick"

A very old principle in magic has been the coin concealed in the hem of a handkerchief. This is an unexpected updating of the classic trick.

THE ILLUSION:

A coin is placed under a handkerchief and given to someone to hold through the cloth. You take a corner, and when you shake out the handkerchief the coin has vanished. And even though they search every inch of the handkerchief, the coin is nowhere to be found!

THE PREPARATION:

You can do this trick only when you're wearing a necktie or a longish scarf around your neck. At the bottom of the tie, or in one corner of the scarf, insert a coin. On some ties and scarves all you will have to do is slit the lining or hem and insert the coin; on others you will have to sew the coin in a small pocket. Tie it around your neck and you're all set (1).

THE TRICK:

Borrow a coin and a handkerchief. Hold the coin in the fingers of your right hand, and as you spread the handkerchief over it, pick up the end of your tie or scarf. Substitute the hidden coin for the borrowed one and let your friend hold it through the cloth of the handkerchief; keep the borrowed coin hidden in your fingers (2). Take two corners of the handkerchief, count to three, and shake the handkerchief out, pulling it from your friend's fingers. This will also pull your hidden coin out of her hand and it will fall down into the original position, right in front of everyone's unsuspecting eyes. Return the borrowed handkerchief, reach in where you keep your loose change, and return the borrowed coin to your friend as one of your own, "to replace her loss . . ."

Three Card Monte

There are two standard versions of the Three Card Monte using faked cards. The other one involves specially printed cards while this one is made with a flap.

THE ILLUSION:

Three cards are shown in a fan and attention directed to the center one. A spectator puts a finger on the back of it and the other two cards are removed, shown, and put aside. When the selected card is turned over it has changed to the Joker.

THE PREPARATION:

Take the Ace of Spades from an old deck and cut it diagonally as shown in the illustration (1). With a small strip of cellophane tape fasten it at an angle on the face of a number card, using the tape as an inside hinge. Now if you put the Joker under the flap, making it match the top and left edges of the flap (2), and place another number card on top of them in a fan shape, it looks as though you have three whole cards (3).

THE TRICK:

Holding the three cards with your thumb covering the lower left corner of the cards, show their faces to your audience. Point out that the Ace is higher in value than the other two and then turn the cards over. Have someone put his finger on the corner of the center card, pushing it down against the table (4). Pull the other two cards away from it and, as you turn them faceup, close them together just enough to hide the Ace of Spades flap. Show him you still have only the two number cards. Ask him to turn over the card under his finger and, Presto!, it has changed to the Joker.

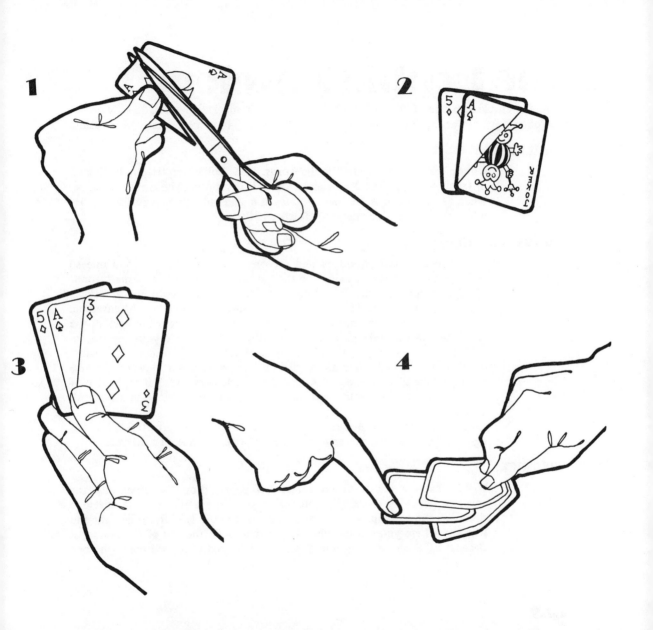

The Double Envelope

A double envelope is one of the most useful secret props in magic. However, do only one of the following tricks at any time—you don't want your friends to suspect what you are using.

THE ILLUSION:

On a piece of paper you write the words: "One dollar" or "Happy Birthday" or (shall we say) "The 3 of Hearts." Seal it in an otherwise empty envelope. When the envelope is cut open, you reach in and pull out an actual one-dollar bill, a birthday card, or the 3 of Hearts itself!

THE PREPARATION:

Take two identical envelopes and set one aside. Hold the second one so you're looking at the flap-side. On the bottom edge make a small mark about 1/32" in from each side. With a razor blade cut on a straight line, at a slight angle, from each mark to the crease of the flap at each end of the envelope. Now cut 1/32" off the bottom of the envelope (1). Discard the back of the envelope and carefully slide the face-and-flap piece inside your second envelope (2). Open the envelope itself, run a thin line of glue, about 1/4" wide, inside the right end. Slide the dollar bill (or card) down between the two flaps, lick the glue on the flap of the real envelope and stick it to the flap of the insert. Now close both flaps together and set the envelope under a book until the glues have dried.

As a precaution, seal shut a third, identical envelope, cut off 1/8" of the right end, and conceal this envelope in your pocket, purse, or a drawer.

THE TRICK:

Write whatever you wish on a piece of paper, drop the paper into the envelope, showing the empty interior as you do so, and seal the envelope shut. Tap the envelope with a pair of scissors. Cut off 1/8" from the right end (the end where you put the line of glue) and open the end of the envelope. Because of the glue, only one of the two compartments will open—the one

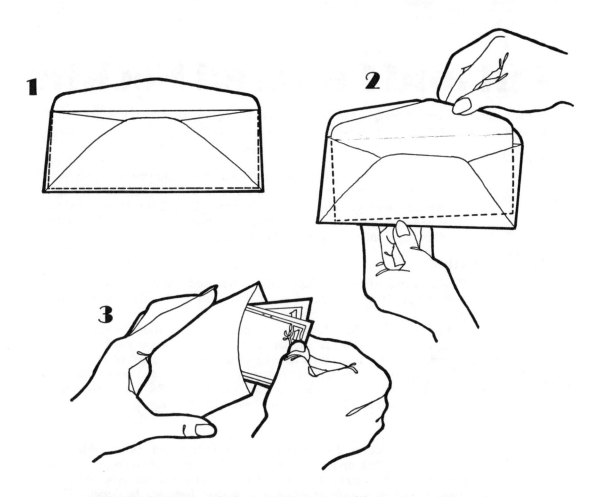

containing whatever you had previously put in it (3). Reach in, pull out the object, and give it to someone. Casually put the envelope in your pocket or purse, and go on to another trick. In case your audience asks to see the envelope, give them the unprepared one, but if they don't ask, don't offer!

Cut and Restored Necktie

In the tradition of comedy magic, this trick has been a long-time favorite. If you like funny situations, this is a good time to use your acting and mugging abilities.

THE ILLUSION:

Someone wearing a necktie is brought forward to help you. Suddenly you accidentally cut off the end of his tie. He removes the tie and, since it's now worthless anyway, you cut it into several more pieces. The remains of the tie are placed in a paper bag, it's blown up, and then burst. You reach into the shreds of paper and remove the necktie completely restored.

THE PREPARATION:

You need one friend, two identical neckties, and two identical paper bags. Your friend is wearing one tie, and the other is secretly hidden in the prepared bag.

Cut one of the bags down each side, about 1" in from the crease, and along the bottom (1). The smaller piece of the bag is now glued inside the second, whole bag by its three cut edges, leaving the top edge open (2). When the glue is dry, put the second necktie in the main compartment of the bag, fold it flat, and have it nearby for when you do the trick. You friend sits in the audience just as if he doesn't know what's going to happen.

THE TRICK:

Mention that you need a helper for your next trick and ask your friend to come forward. Pick up a pair of scissors and tell everyone you're going to do a cut-and-restored string trick that is absolutely marvelous. Ask him if he happens to have a piece of string in his pocket. Naturally he doesn't. Then notice that he apparently has a spot on the end of his tie. Ask him if he knows how to remove the spot and when he says, "No," cut off the end of the tie. At this point he should act as though he can't believe what you've just done, but you tell him you can fix it. He removes his necktie and reluctantly

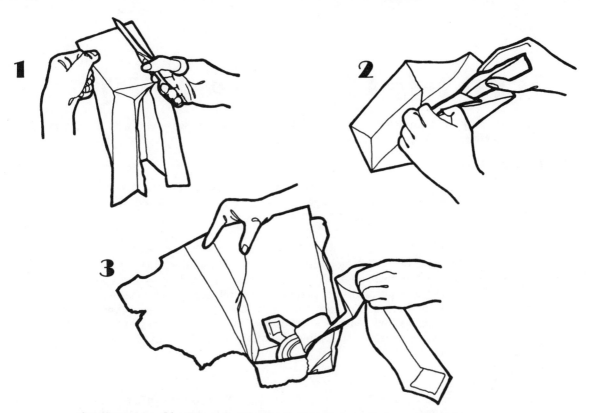

gives it to you. You immediately cut it into five or six more pieces, open up the paper bag, and place the pieces inside. However, you don't place them in the main part of the bag. You have slid your finger in between the two false sides of the bag so the pieces can go into the secret compartment. Have your friend blow up the bag, then you reach over and burst it. Because the two sides of the secret compartment are glued together, they are strong enough to withstand the popping. Only the single side in the main part will break open. Reach inside the torn bag and remove the whole necktie, letting the audience see the empty interior of the bag as you do so (3). As your helper knots the whole tie around his neck, casually wad up the bag and put it away.

The two of you must act as though the first cutting of the necktie is a bad joke on your part, and, of course, your friend must be loyal enough to never tell how you actually did the trick.

Torn and Restored Bill

There are many ways to restore a torn bill, but this method will leave you with a bill that can be examined, and it involves no sleight of hand.

THE ILLUSION:

A bill is shown on both sides, torn in half a number of times, and the pieces placed under someone's finger. A magic phrase is uttered, and when the bill is removed and unfolded, it is whole once again!

THE PREPARATION:

You need two matching bills in fairly new condition. Without creasing it first, tear one of them in half, down through the center. As you look at the portrait side, put the right-hand half of the bill in a safe place until later. Fold the second bill in half, down through the center, and, with rubber cement, stick the half-bill on the edge of the fold of the whole bill so the two half-patterns match (1). Unfold the whole bill underneath and press it flat to the half-bill covering it.

THE TRICK:

Remove the bill from your wallet, holding the two right ends together. Show the bill front and back; it looks like one bill if you don't slow down long enough for anyone to compare the two serial numbers. Hold the bill in front of you with the portrait towards your audience and fold the right ends back towards you and over to the left. <u>Crease the bill down the center and then apparently open the bill again.</u> What you actually do is unfold, just the half-bill, back to the right (2). Hold the top edge in both hands on each side of the center and tear the right half away from you to separate the rubber cement. It will make a tearing sound very close to an actual rip, and you will have what looks like a "half" in each hand. Put the right half in front of the left (that is, on the audience's side) and then fold the two right edges back

(Continued)

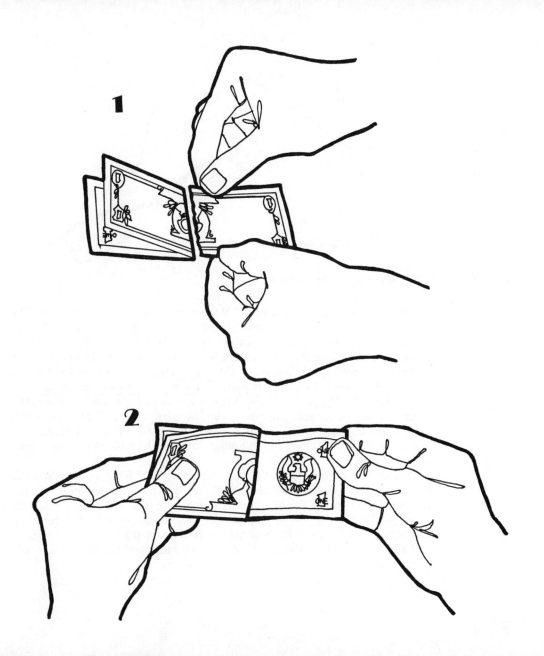

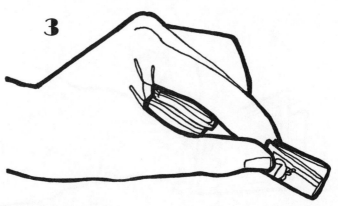

(TORN AND RESTORED BILL, continued)

towards you and to the left again. Make a crease and, once again from the back, open out just the single half. Tear it down along the crease of the real bill. Separate your hands, then put the right piece in front of the left bundle. Turn the bundle a quarter-turn to the left (counterclockwise) and repeat the process for another tear. Again put the right piece in front of the left bundle, cupping the bundle in your left hand. <u>Look at one of your friends and ask him to hold the bill on the table.</u> As your left hand turns down and puts the pieces on the table, your thumb pushes outward on the folded whole bill, leaving the torn pieces hidden in the left fingers (3). Your friend puts his index finger on the folded bill to hold it down on the table as you draw your left hand back.

Ask him to say the words, "Novus ordo seclorum." When he does, you ask him if he knows the phrase, and he will say, "No." Tell him it's in one of the circles on the back of the bill, and he should give you that piece of the bill. When he lifts his finger and opens the bill, he will now find it restored. Meanwhile you have put the real pieces either in your lap or in your pocket.

Later, you can tape the pieces of the torn bill together and turn it in to a bank for a new bill. Practice with play money.

12

Party Magic

Party Magic

HOW TO GIVE A MAGIC SHOW AT YOUR (OR A KID'S) BIRTHDAY PARTY
"Birthdays are magic days. . . !"

THE SHOW:

Stepping before your expectant audience you place a large box on the table. Slowly you unwrap the ribbon and stretch it out to its full length. Doubling it up you find the center and cut it with a pair of scissors. You clip off pieces from the two new ends to prove the ribbon really has been cut. You then make uncutting motions with the scissors and when you unfold the ribbon it has been restored to its one long length.

Again the ribbon is cut in half, and each end of one half is tied around a wrist of a guest. The second length is looped through the first person's ribbon and then each end is tied around a wrist of a second person, so the two are linked. The challenge is for the two "prisoners" to free themselves from each other, but without untying the ribbons. When all their efforts have gone for naught, you step forward and, with a few quick moves, you free them.

Now the paper is removed from the box, folded into a triangular shape, and you begin tearing small pieces from it. When you finally unfold the paper, you have made a beautiful and intricate lace design.

The inside of the box is shown to be empty, except for the small pieces you dropped in as you were tearing the design. The lid is put on top, and the entire audience shouts the magic words. When the box is opened again, there is a box of crayons inside.

A guest and you now do a trick together. While your back is turned, the guest goes into the audience and has a crayon selected. It is put in your hand and the box is closed to hide the other crayons. Turning to face your audience, you start thinking very deeply. Suddenly, you name the color and then show the crayon to prove it.

(Continued)

THE PREPARATION:

You will need:

> Box at least 6″ square and with a top-fitting lid
> Spool of thread and a needle
> Pair of scissors
> Roll of solid-colored gift wrapping paper, not tissue
> Roll of satin ribbon at least 1/2″ wide, of contrasting color to the paper
> Bottle of rubber cement

Take a length of thread three-quarters the width of the lid and tie a knot in one end. Thread the other end about an inch through a needle and push the needle up all the way through one edge of the lid where the back meets the top and halfway between the two sides. Push the needle back through the edge about 1/2″ from your first hole. Remove the needle from the thread, tie a large knot that won't slip through the hole, and then pull your thread tight on the inside. Put an ink dot on top of the lid where your thread is fastened. Open the box of crayons, lay the thread across the two little ears that are folded in on each side, and close the top. Pull the knot in the end of the thread up against the side of the box and it should stay secure. The box of crayons should hang in the center of the lid if you hold the lid vertically (1).

Put the lid on the box, with the crayons inside. Measure around the box in the direction you're going to wrap it. Add 2″ to your figure and then cut a square piece of wrapping paper that size. Fold the square diagonally with the color to the inside (2). Fold the resulting triangle in half (3). Now fold this triangle into thirds (4). Lightly mark the back panel with the design shown in the drawing; the shaded parts will be the pieces you'll tear out when you do the show (5). Make a couple of extras and practice on them so you can do the routine smoothly.

(Continued)

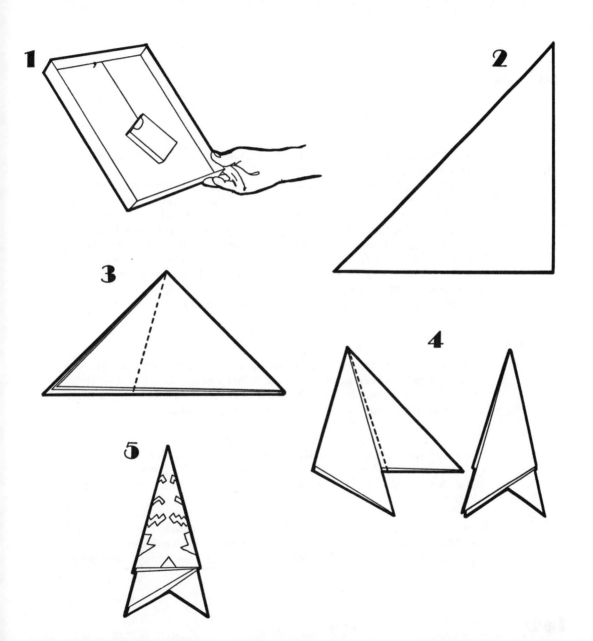

Unfold the paper and wrap the box. You may have to fold in one edge to make it fit neatly—just don't cut it!

Cut a length of ribbon seven feet long and stretch it out in front of you. Cut another piece about 5″ long and, with the rubber cement, glue it to the center of the longer ribbon. Cement only about 1/2″ of each end of the short piece to the long ribbon (6). When you put the long ribbon around the box, just make sure to have the short piece on the inside of the ribbon next to the box so it won't be seen. Put the long ribbon around the box in a decorative manner to use up the entire length. Make a bow from a separate piece of ribbon and tie that to the package.

Have a pair of scissors handy when you are ready to do the show, and you're all set.

THE SHOW:

Arrange with the hostess of the party that you will present your package after all the others have been opened, because it has a magic show that goes along with it. When it's time, have the birthday child sit in the center of the front row as you step in front of your audience with your package.

"This is a very special present because what is inside will give you lots of fun for years to come. Also, it will give all of us a lot of fun right now. First of all, here is the bow to remind you of this magic present as well as the magic of having so many friends with you on your birthday."

Untie the bow and give it to the day's star and then unwrap the ribbon. Run the ribbon through your hand until you come to the extra piece in the center. Separate it from the ribbon by pulling the center of it up through your fist as

(Continued)

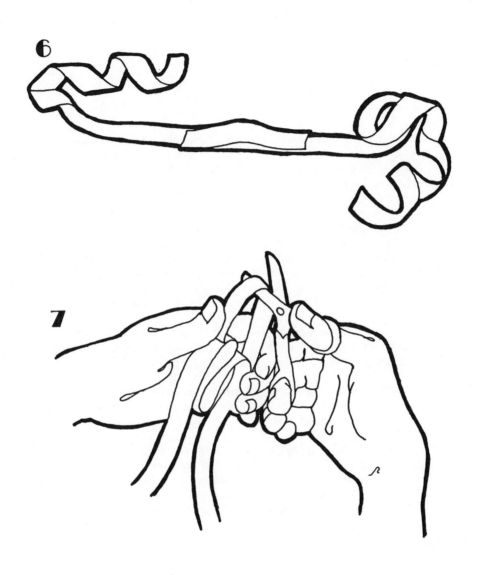

though it's the center of the ribbon, leaving the real center hidden in your fist (7). Cut the center of the extra piece, then cut small pieces from the two new ends until you get down to where they're cemented to the long ribbon. Hold the scissors high in the air.

> "Now that I have thoroughly chopped up the center of the ribbon I want to teach you a very handy skill with scissors. This (you open the scissors with a jerk, and close them slowly) is known to magicians as 'uncutting with scissors.' There are also ways to uncut with a knife and an electric shaver, but since we used scissors I'll just teach you this one for now. What you do is uncut with the scissors over the ribbon (do so), and you automatically repair the damage."

Give each outer end of the ribbon to a child and have them pull it out of your fist to show that it is restored. Put a hand on each side of the center and jerk the ribbon a couple of times to show its strength.

> "Now I need two smart volunteers. How about you—and you—coming up here to help me. You see, they were smart enough to not volunteer and that's a good start."

As the two children are coming forward you take the ribbon and cut it in the center, then trim the ends to get rid of the part with the cement on it. Take one of the lengths and tie one end loosely around each wrist of one of the children. The second length is tied around a wrist of the second child, threaded through the loop of the other ribbon, and tied to the other wrist (8).

(Continued)

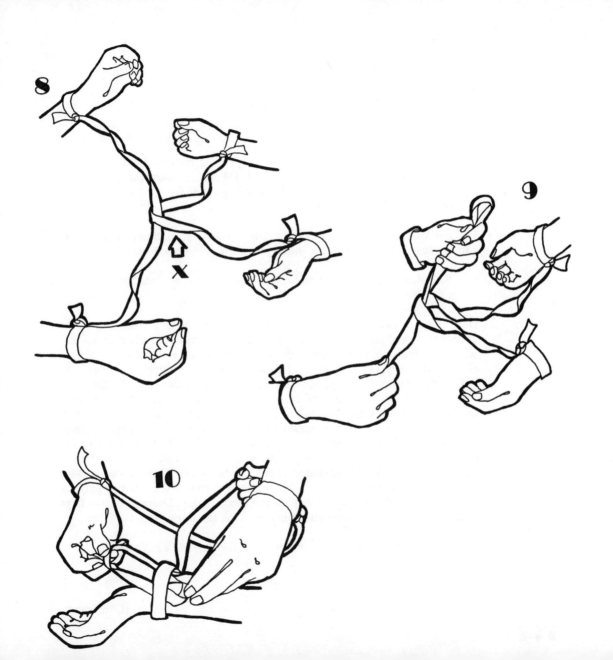

"Now you'll notice that the two of you are now tied together—or didn't you want to be married? Well, I'll tell you something. If you think very hard you might find a way to get free from each other. Do any of the rest of you have any ideas?"

Let the kids try to manipulate the ribbons to free themselves, with and without help, until you feel the mood just starting to slow down.

"All right, let me show you how, in case you ever get into this kind of a fix again."

Double the center of one of the ribbons. Now look to see which end of the other person's ribbon comes *over* this ribbon (X), and take the loop to that wrist (9). Push that loop through the circlet which is around the second child's wrist (10), over his hand (11), and back down through the circlet (12). Pull on the ends of the loop, and the ribbons will drop free of each other.

Reseat all your helpers and then remove the paper from the box, turning the box so your ink mark on the lid is at the back, away from your audience. Refold the paper along the creases so you again have your triangular shape with your pencil pattern on your side of the paper. Lift the lid of the box just enough so you can push it forward about 3". Start tearing out the pattern in the paper and dropping the pieces inside the box (13). "I don't want to be a litterbug, you know." When all the pieces are removed from the pattern, carefully open the paper and display the fancy design. Drape it over a large chair or on the back of a couch while you finish the show (14).

"Now, what everyone's been waiting for—to see what's inside the box."

(Continued)

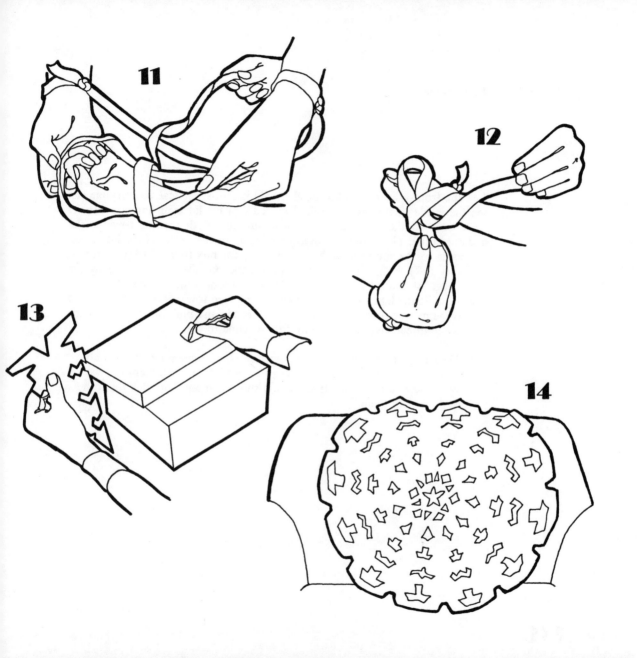

Lift the front edge of the lid, until the lid is almost vertical, so everyone can see the inside of it **(15)**. Drop the front edge of the lid again and now lift the back edge so the lid is again vertical but now with the top towards the audience **(16)**. The crayons should be hanging in the center of the lid but on your side so the audience can't see them. Tip the box forward to show that it is empty **(17)**. Bring the box back upright and put the lid on, dropping the front edge of the lid on first **(18)**. Have everyone yell, "Happy Birthday," then you lift the lid and carry it forward, top tilted towards the audience, and lean it against the front of the box **(19)**. Reach in and pull the crayons off the end of the thread and hold them up for everyone to see.

"There you are, your magic present. Just remember, they only appeared by magic, you still have to color pictures with them the way everyone else does. But first, let me show you another trick that can be done with them."

(Continued)

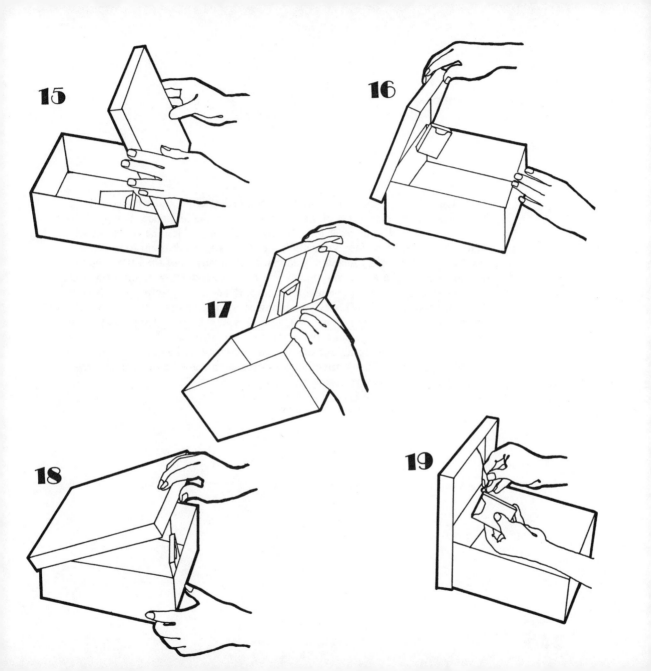

15

16

17

18

19

Give the box of opened crayons to the birthday child and turn your back while one of the crayons is chosen and shown to the audience. It's put into your hand behind your back and the box is closed to hide the other crayons (20). Turn around to face your audience, and as you ask them to think very hard on the color they selected, you mark the fingernail of the little finger of the hand not holding the crayon. As you begin to concentrate, you bring out that hand, making sure the audience can see it's definitely empty, and hold it to your forehead (21). Think for a moment with your eyes closed, then tell them you have it. Open your eyes, and as you take your hand away from your forehead, quickly name the color on your fingernail. Repeat the name of the color and then bring out the crayon in your other hand and return it to the birthday child. Thank them all for being such a good audience, and then send them off for their refreshments.

KNOT AS I DO

THE ILLUSION:

You hand someone one length of ribbon and you take another, holding one end in each hand. Looping yours around your hands, with your helper duplicating every move, and without letting go of the ends, you manage to tie a knot in the center of your ribbon. Unfortunately, your helper fails! And fails every time, no matter how slowly you show your audience.

THE TRICK:

Loop the right end of the ribbon over your left wrist for about half its length (22). Then following the pattern shown in the drawing, thread your right hand through that loop, behind the vertical strand, and back out through the loop (23). Pull the ribbon taut between your two hands and with the knuckles of your fists towards the floor (24). Stop there to make sure your helper has made the same moves as you did. Now turn both fists in towards each other and as you pull them out of the loops the right fingers secretly drop their end and grab the ribbon at point A (25). When the loops fall away from your hands there is an overhand knot in the center of your ribbon.

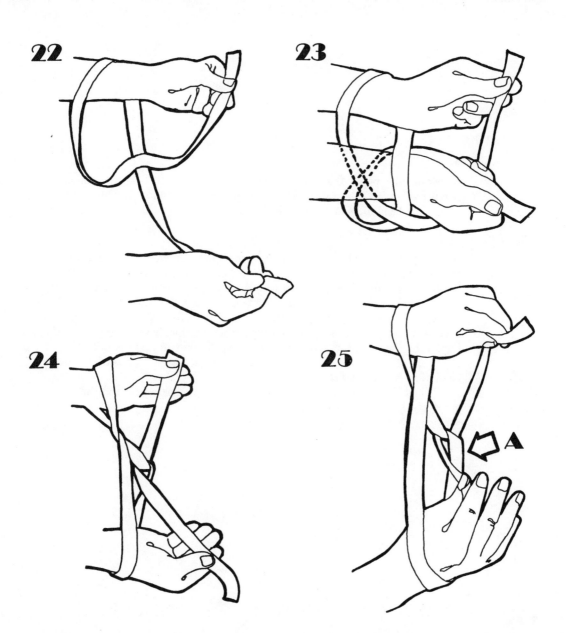

THE BIRTHDAY CAP

THE ILLUSION:

Removing the paper from the package you tear it into a smaller square. A number of quick folds, and you have a genuine old-fashioned soldier's hat to put on the head of the birthday child.

THE TRICK:

Before you wrapped the box in the paper you turned the paper over and marked the uncolored side in a 2-to-1 ratio so you know where to tear out the rectangle later. When you get to this stunt at the party tear the paper into its shape. Fold it in half, bringing the two ends together (26). Fold down the two creased corners onto the same side, and then fold up the edges on each side (27). Open it up in the opposite direction, tucking the corners of the flaps into the opposite sides (28). Fold up the bottom points until they're about 2" short of the top point (29). Open out the hat and drop it on the head of its lucky owner.

"I also do weddings, swimming pool dedications, and ash tray emptyings!"

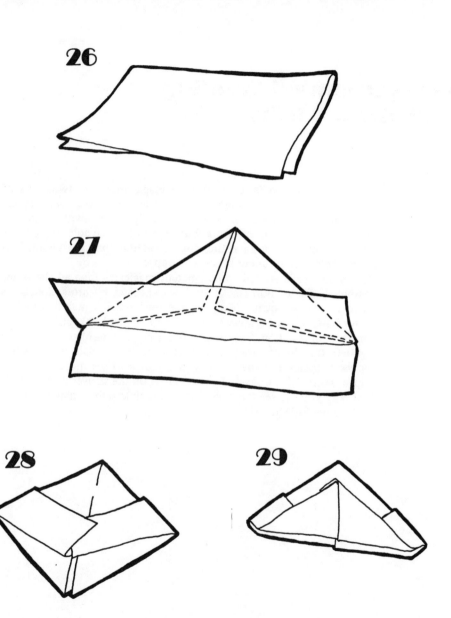

Recommended Reading and Magic Clubs

If you're interested in learning more magic there are two areas of further information, other magicians and libraries. The best way to find other magicians is to contact the nearest magic shop. The owner might even have a magic club meeting in his store, but at least he'll be able to introduce you to other amateurs if not an entire club. Look him up in the Yellow Pages of the telephone directory under Magician's Supplies.

Libraries have started more amateur magicians than all the other sources combined. Their book stacks are even checked by professionals when they arrive in a new town. Being on the road for the majority of the year, a professional doesn't always hear about the latest book, and a library can give him that information. The following is a good starter list for you after having digested this book. They are all for beginners and will teach the very necessary basics and then help you progress to the more involved tricks. A helpful hint: All the magic books will be on the shelves in the 793.8 section. That way you can see them all at the same time rather than going through the card file one title at a time.

Blackstone, Harry, *Blackstone's Modern Card Tricks and Secrets of Magic*

Elliott, Bruce, *The Best in Magic; Classic Secrets of Magic; Magic as a Hobby; Professional Magic Made Easy*

Gibson, Walter, *Professional Magic for Amateurs*

Hay, Henry, *Learn Magic*

Hugard, Jean, *Modern Magic Manual*

Hugard & Braue, *Royal Road to Card Magic*

Kaye, Marvin, *The Stein and Day Handbook of Magic*

Scarne, John, *Scarne on Card Tricks; Scarne's Magic Tricks*

Severn, Bill, *Bill Severn's Big Book of Magic*

Tarbell, Harlan, *Tarbell Course in Magic* (7 volumes)

Thurston, Howard, *400 Tricks You Can Do*

There are two major magic clubs from which additional information may be obtained. One is The Society of American Magicians (Herbert B. Downs, National Secretary, 66 Marked Tree Road, Needham, Mass. 02192) and the other is The International Brotherhood of Magicians (Kenton, Ohio—no street address necessary). Membership in these organizations entitles you to receive their regularly issued magazines.

Magician's Certificate

_____ ,

THE GREAT

Having Completed & Mastered the Effects of

MAGIC FOR NON-MAGICIANS,

Has now Graduated from the rank of non-magician to one of

AMATEUR MAGICIAN;

And promises to *keep secret* the Effects learned,

To Respect the tricks of Professional Magic,

To practice & perfect the Art, to

the Mystification & Amusement

of his friends & compeers;

And to spread the Joy & Happiness gotten from a

Newly Acquired Skill.

AWARDED BY:

Shari Lewis

Shari Lewis

Abraham B. Hurwitz

Abraham B. Hurwitz